The Sanford Meisner Approach

WORKBOOK THREE
tackling the text

Smith and Kraus *Books For Actors*

CAREER DEVELOPMENT: Technique

CAREER DEVELOPMENT: Actor's Guides

If you require prepublication information about upcoming Smith and Kraus books, you may receive our semiannual catalogue, free of charge, by sending your name and address to *Smith and Kraus Catalogue, P.O. Box 127, Lyme, NH 03768. Or call us at (800) 895-4331, fax (603) 643-1831.*

The Sanford Meisner Approach

WORKBOOK THREE
tackling the text

Larry Silverberg

Career Development Series

A SMITH AND KRAUS BOOK

Published by Smith and Kraus, Inc.
PO Box 127, Lyme, NH 03768
Copyright ©1998 by Larry Silverberg
Manufactured in the United States of America
Cover and Text Design by Julia Hill

First Edition: July 1998
10 9 8 7 6 5 4 3

The Library of Congress Cataloging-In-Publication Data

Silverberg, Larry, 1959–
    The Sanford Meisner approach: workbook three: tackling the text / by Larry Silverberg.

    p. cm. (A career development book)
    ISBN 1-57525-130-2

    1. Drama—Explication. 2. Meisner, Sanford. I. Title.
    PN1707.S46   1998
    808.2—dc21   98-23061
                    CIP

acknowledgments

Thank you God for the health and energy to keep working.

Thank you to my wife Jill and my two inspired children, Sarah and Aaron!

Thank you to the two teachers who lit my acting fire, Sandy Meisner and Suzanne Shepherd.

Thank you to all of my family in Florida who check in on me once a week to see if I am still sane.

Thank you to my dearest friend, Dick Kowal, whose enthusiasm for all of my accomplishments and whose ear for my struggles is so continually healing.

Thank you Marisa and Eric, my dear friends and publishers for their sense of humor and their faith in me.

Thank you to Julia whose gifted eye gives these books the looks!

Thanks to Horton Foote and William Mastrosimone for your beautiful plays and for permitting me to make you such an important part of this book.

Thanks to all my current students in my Meisner Actors Training Program '98 at my theatre here in Seattle (The Belltown Theatre Center) for your dedication and commitment to the work — and for being so much fun!

Thank you to all the wonderful people who have so generously supported my theatre this last year including Sydney Pollack, Donna Ostroff, Teri Mathews, Terry Joyner, our anonymous donor who has made a whole year of programming possible, our board of directors, April Shawhan for coming to Seattle to direct *American Buffalo* and the countless volunteers who love our busy little artistic home.

Thank you to Renee Basinger in Atlanta for caring so much; your students are very lucky to have you.

And, thank you to all of my readers for your interest and your kind words about my books.

For My Son,
Aaron

T a c k l i n g   t h e   T e x t

contents

preface

One of the biggest thrills and stimulants for me as an actor has been the opportunity to collaborate with playwrights. Amazingly, this process can occur whether the writer is alive or dead, present or absent. I have been fortunate enough to have brought my craft to the genius of playwrights from Shakespeare to Tennessee Williams – from Henrik Ibsen to David Mamet – from August Stringberg to Athol Fugard.

From the beginning of my career I have been in awe of playwrights who can mine their life experiences and then through whatever magical or alchemical process, refine that rough ore into a play. I learned early that such a transformation is not simply an intellectual process. Experience must be distilled and then subjected to the intense heat generated by the writer's passion to fashion a world. A world which serves as a metaphor for his personal experience.

I have come to believe that if we as actors want to enter and participate and contribute to that world, we must dare to feed the fire of the author's vision with our most personal inner heat. If that requires courage, trust, even recklessness, so be it. In *Tackling the Text,* Larry Silverberg opens the door to such a process and invites us to step inside.

I recently had the good fortune to direct Larry Silverberg, Laurason Driscoll and Shayn Bjornholm in the Belltown Theatre Center's production of *American Buffalo,* written by a former Sanford Meisner student, David Mamet. As you probably know, the play is set in a junk shop, Don's Resale. The first day of rehearsal we sat around the usual bare table on the usual bare stage and did our first reading of the text. In my experience, the first reading can be a disastrous (at best, wasteful) exercise in showing-off our acting "brilliance" when it is our turn to speak and evaluating the other actor's lack of same when they spoke. Or it can be the beginning of an exploration and understanding of our colleagues in relation to the text. We chose to explore. Day after day, we searched for ways to surrender to the immediacy of each others presence and to the incredible richness and density of Mr. Mamet's verbalized journey. Our bare stage wasn't bare for long. Objects of all sizes and sometimes inscrutable purpose were brought like offerings by actors, stage management and technical staff. Then tables had to be found to display these "treasures." And soon, the actor's were creating a world for themselves with the swiftly accumulating "stuff." One day Larry brought in a deck of cards and taught himself how to play solitaire with the fierceness and desperation of a gambler on a never ending losing streak. Laurason discovered an old broom and a handleless dustpan. In no time he was finding Don's satisfaction in maintaining some sense of order and control over the developing sense of "place." I suppose it was inevitable that Larry, as Teach, trying to ingratiate himself with Donny, would snatch the dust pan and stoop to receive the dusty deposits of Donny's broom. Suddenly activities were not illustrations or gestures — but actions. The actors were not merely coming from offstage to onstage, but were entering work. A refuge from the rain, the dark, the uncaring, the violent. A world that could evoke in a quick succession a sense of belonging, of isolation, of fantasy, or abject failure. We spent a lot of time working on emotional preparation. Through improvisation, through trial and error we worked to be ever more specific about the life of each character prior to the encounter of each scene. I found myself working more and more one-on-one with the actors. I would give them their notes and discuss their work problems privately. This is not my usual way of working, but I found it helped create surprises and spontaneity during rehearsals. It worked as a challenge, even a kind of game for the actors to recognize and accept the new things their partners would try out. A strong sense of "play" became an organic part of our work. To quote Sanford Meisner, "Now, play, play! It's a play."

I encourage you to read, explore and enjoy *Tackling the Text*. Before going to Seattle to direct *American Buffalo*, I read

Larry's first two Meisner textbooks. They made me feel I knew him and that we would become friends. When Larry writes, it is as if he is talking directly to you. You feel in personal touch with his enthusiasm, his positiveness, his passion and his insight. Take it from me, it's a good feeling.

Sanford Meisner once said, "It takes years to be an actor." Where ever you are on that journey, I'm sure this book will be a helpful companion for you. In Tennessee Williams' *Camino Real*, the character of Byron announces before he heads alone across a seemingly endless desert, "Make voyages. Attempt them. There's nothing else." Bon voyage.

April Shawhan

introduction

Welcome to Workbook Three, our class on how to approach working with a playwright's script. The foundation work we have done together in Workbook One and Workbook Two has strengthened you in essential ways and has prepared you for incorporating these next crucial elements into your own *very personal* craft of acting. (Oh, by the way, If you haven't read my first two Meisner books, you may go ahead and read this book and I invite you to take a look at books one and two as it will make your experience here much more rewarding.)

To be brief, (so we can get to work!) I want you to know that this book is about three primary things related to working with the text and acting the part —

1. Freeing your instincts

Using the exercises in books one and two, you re-claimed your instinctual self! You re-ignited the part of you that is fully expressive, fully present and available, immediately responsive, spontaneous, passionate, emotionally alive, keenly interested and human. You learned how to bring a simplicity and a reality to the stage that is extraordinary and rare.

Now, how do you bring all of that wonderful life and aliveness to the text? Well, in a step-by-step fashion—that's what we will be working on in the following lessons. Sound good?

2. Reading the script like an actor

Let me describe it this way. After graduating from the Neighborhood Playhouse and studying with Sandy, I was most fortunate to continue my studies with Suzanne Shepherd. Suzanne gave me so much and one of the most important things was how to investigate the script like an x-ray. That's a great analogy, looking at the script "like an x-ray."

My best buddy, Richard Kowal, who is an extraordinary chiropractor and nutritionist in New York City, described looking at x-rays to me. He said that on his, or *anyone's,* first look — the person's basic skeleton is immediately apparent. Then, he takes a second, more careful look and through his *trained eyes,* he can see how each of the bones relate to the others. And as he continues to look, certain elements of particular bones, (such as size, shape and density,) will "speak" to him and he begins to see these specific parts in the context of the whole skeleton and in the context of what he knows about the person who was x-rayed.

As you noticed, I highlighted the words "anyone" and "trained eyes." Obviously, anyone can read a play and the basic storyline will be immediately apparent. But you are not anyone, you are the actor reading the script and it is vital that you train your "eyes" to "see" the script in a deeper and more specific way. We are talking about refining your sensibilities to the text! It is only when you have become sensitized to:

- the characters in the play and how they respond to each other;
- how the characters relate to the world around them;
- the pivotal circumstances the characters find themselves in;
- how the characters react to these circumstances and
- the specific point of view of each character,

that the script will begin to "speak" to you in a very personal way. And, listen now, getting on intimate terms with the script is key.

3. Having Fun!

Ultimately, ULTIMATELY, it's gotta be fun. Don't you think? I mean, if it's not, why would we go through all the difficulties and hard work necessary to do this thing called acting. And, as with any true craft, the process is demanding and rigorous and uncomfortable. But you know what? I have found that even that which may be uncomfortable now, becomes enjoyable. Even when I go through that period of terror that has no end in sight until I suddenly find I am on the other side, when I look back at it — hey, I was having fun! (I don't know, maybe I have a strange concept of fun?)

But listen, acting is fun and when you do it for real, as we have been so meticulously working on together, it becomes glorious! The hard work comes first, then you leave the work alone and what's left is pure fun.

So, let's get to it...

Section One
it's not about the words

exploring

It's not about the words. Does that sound like a strange way to begin a book that's all about "tackling the text"? Isn't the text, the script, made up of words?

Let's go back, for a moment, and discuss some issues we raised in our early sessions together. I want to alert you here, once again, to our true job as actors. I believe, if we want to speak in the most simple way, our job as actors is to bring life to the stage. Now that's certainly a big deal. I am talking about LIFE! ALIVENESS! And, that's exactly what everything we have worked on together in the first two books has been in aim of. Bringing life to the stage, SOUL: *"That, which is in us, is most human."* I mean, if we're going to make some theatre, let's make it theatre that's alive!

If we used an automobile as an analogy, I would say that with the parts of the Meisner process we have worked on thus far, we have been working mostly on the "fuel supply." And now, in book three, we are going to make the transition into the building of the engine. Remember, we need both. You get that? We may have plenty of fuel but, listen, you want that car to really take you places? Then you better have a well built engine to put all that gas in.

So, if it's not about the words, what is it about?

It's about knowing. Let me explain. The words are only a small nugget of what really communicates from the stage. By the way, same thing in life. How many times have you been with a person and felt that what they were saying did not reveal what they were really thinking or feeling. How many times have you been with a person and walked away knowing that what you said did not reveal what YOU were really thinking or feeling. I want you to take some time to complete the following writing assignments:

. . .

Write about an encounter in which you felt that the person did not reveal what they were truly thinking or feeling. What did they say and what did you think or feel was really going on underneath all the words?

_____

_____

_____

_____

_____

_____

_____

_____

_____

_____

_____

_____

_____

_____

_____

_____

_____

_____

_____

_____

_____

Write about an encounter in which you did not reveal what you were truly thinking or feeling. What did you say and what was really going on underneath all of your words?

_____

_____

_____

_____

_____

_____

_____

_____

_____

_____

_____

_____

_____

_____

_____

_____

_____

_____

_____

_____

. . .

I am suggesting to you that what communicates has to do with what we truly "know" and with meaning, personal meaning. Sandy used to say to us, *It's never about showing. It's always about knowing.*" Unfortunately, most actors don't understand this and so most of their energy is spent in an attempt to illustrate the words. What do I mean by "illustrating." Another way of saying it is, "making it look like." Here's an example. You are in a play and the following line is your character's only line. I want you to read it outloud:

Hey, go get me a peanut butter sandwich because I love peanut butter!!

Now, if you're like just about every other person I have asked to say that line, you discovered yourself emphasizing the word *love* as you said "...because I L-O-V-E peanut butter!" Whether you actually love peanut butter or not isn't the point. The thing is, your mind will always lead you to the cliche of how you think a line should be performed. We see an exclamation point and we think the line should be read a certain way. We see a question mark and we think the line should be read a certain way. We have to say "I love you" and so we think we should act a certain way. You are playing the part of a mother so you think you have to act motherly. BULLSHIT! You get that? It's not true in life, is it? Are all mothers "motherly?"

Illustrating or, "making it look like," is always a lie. It's an actor's attempt to look good and to force the audience to like her or him. But you cannot force an audience to do anything. And they will know — no matter how good a liar you are — that you are faking it. And they will leave the play with nothing more than they came with. In fact, they will leave with less because you just stole two hours of their life from them. What a waste.

Are you starting to get the feeling that I believe there is an urgency here; an urgency to learn an approach to working with text that will empower you to bring to the play the kind of life you have started to discover in the foundation exercises from my books one and two? Well, you're right, I do believe it is urgent. As Suzanne said to us, "Theatre isn't casual, it's *EMERGENCY! EMERGENCY! EMERGENCY!*"

I want to make even clearer what I mean when I say it is about "knowing." First of all, I do not mean the kind of knowing in *"Well, I know my lines, don't I?"* Lot's of people will say to you, *"My goodness, how do you remember all those lines?"* Certainly, learning the words, even if it's tough for you, is the least of your acting challenges. You simply put in the time and somehow you get it done. (Later, I will talk about ways to help you learn the words.) No, when I speak of knowing, I am talking about another domain entirely.

Here are a few writing exercises for you to continue to explore the kind of "knowing" I am speaking about. As you respond, get as specific as you can — try to put down every detail that you can remember.

· · ·

Write about something someone once did for you which made you feel really happy.

_____

_____

_____

_____

_____

_____

_____

_____

_____

_____

_____

_____

_____

_____

_____

_____

_____

_____

_____

_____

_____

Write about something one of your parents once did that made you extremely angry.

_____

_____

_____

_____

_____

_____

_____

_____

_____

_____

_____

_____

_____

_____

_____

_____

_____

_____

_____

_____

_____

Write about a time you got very excited.

_____

_____

_____

_____

_____

_____

_____

_____

_____

_____

_____

_____

_____

_____

_____

_____

_____

_____

_____

_____

_____

_____

Write about a time you were very scared.

_____

_____

_____

_____

_____

_____

_____

_____

_____

_____

_____

_____

_____

_____

_____

_____

_____

_____

_____

_____

_____

. . .

As an example, I'll share with you just a bit of my own response to one of the writing assignments.

I remember the horror and shock, nine years ago, of being told by my mother at the hospital that, this time, Grandma wasn't going to come home, that she was going to die within a few days. On one of those last few days, I was in Grandma's hospital room and I was sitting by her side, holding her left hand. She was being given morphine to ease the terrible pain she was in and she was hallucinating. She was yelling, louder than I had ever heard her yell, about sewing needles and pleading for someone to save Sheila (her daughter and my mother.) I kept trying to calm her but it was no use. I was panicking inside and trying to hold it together so I could help Grandma. I clung to her hand and rubbed her arm and told her that Sheila was okay. At some point, Grandma became quiet and closed her eyes.

I was very scared; would she open her eyes again? Is she still breathing? I sat there holding her hand and looked at the blue veins and her soft, tan skin and I realized that I had never really seen her hands before, not really. I sat and thought about how these hands had spent a lifetime cooking, cleaning, and knitting for all of us and taking care of my sisters and me. I thought of the photo of her bathing me with a washcloth when I was a newborn. I remembered the time in the backyard when I was seven and I was acting nutty and I threw a ball wildly and it landed on Grandma's finger, bending it back-

wards and making Grandma cry in pain and how I ran into my room and cried because I made Grandma cry...

Something else happened a few moments later. It's a great example of how surprising life is and how every event is filled with infinite possibility; that no event fits into the narrow confines of the storybook cliches we make up in our minds or see on T.V.

As I said, Grandma had just become quiet and had closed her eyes. I was terrified that she might die at that very moment. Then, the elderly and very ill woman who was in the bed directly across from Grandma began to scream, "I DON'T LIKE THIS TRIP, I DON'T LIKE THIS TRIP, THIS ISN'T A GOOD TRIP!" With her eyes still closed, Grandma suddenly yelled back, as if she was reminding the woman of a widely known fact, "Save your receipt, they'll give it all back to you!" I burst out laughing, so hard my sides hurt. In the midst of what was really happening, it was a most amazing moment, don't you think?

So, what's the point of all this? The point is that when we speak about our lives and about what's important to us, we speak from what we truly know. The meaning of that information lives in us. We don't have to think about what to say, we say it. And, as we talk, we have a direct and intimate relationship with the things we are talking about. Also, the meaning of what we are talking about has an impact on us that is out of our control. This is the kind of "knowing" that I have been referring to. Because, you know what? It's the same for every character in every play. When they speak, they speak from a personal knowing. And somehow, SOMEHOW, it is your job as the actor to make those character's words, the words that you have to speak, *your own;* you will have to make those words something you really "know" about. (I'm planting seeds right now. I am planting seeds. Get that?)

Well, enough said. Let's move into actually working with the script.

Section Two

encountering the text

reading the scene

I am now going to give you your first scene. Are you excited? (I am!) The scene is a two person scene for one man and one woman.

Important! Please do not read the scene until you have the time to read it by yourself in a quiet place where there are no distractions. Make sure you are not in a rush to get somewhere else or do something else. And, when you do read the scene, *do not* read it out loud.

As you can see, I am suggesting that your first reading of the script is an important event. Careful now! As you read, your head will immediately begin to figure everything out. But you must resist the temptation to act the scene out in your mind; you must refrain from any form of rehearsing how the scene should go or how the lines should be "delivered." I am asking you to read the scene to yourself and, as best you can, simply listen. Listen to the words and allow them to do what they do to you.

If you don't have quiet and private time right now, put the book down and come back to it later.

. . .

You're ready to read? Good, here is your scene:

The Legend of Sarah by James Gow and Arnaud d'Usseau
The Characters: Adam Harwick and Minerva Pinney

Adam: What in God's name do you think you're doing?

Minerva: I'm packing! Don't you have any eyes in your head? I'm packing!

Adam: Well, you can stop packing! Stop it right now!

Minerva: Out of my way!

Adam: You're being ridiculous! It's late and hotels are expensive.

Minerva: I'm not going to a hotel, I'm going home.

Adam: Good grief! Home to mother! Minerva Pinney returns to mama and the ancestral homestead! You disappoint me darling. This started out as a good honest row — but now you're being commonplace.

Minerva: I'm not your darling and I never want to see you again and please go in the other room!

Adam: And don't cry! In the name of heaven, don't cry! Tears will get you nowhere. You merely look messy.

Minerva: Adam, why didn't you pay the light bill? I gave you the money.

Adam: How many times do I have to tell you? I forgot! I completely forgot!

Minerva: But you spent the money.

Adam: Of course I spent the money. If I find ten dollars in my pocket and I need books, I buy the books. What's wrong with that? Besides I can take them out of my income tax.

Minerva: What income? You can't even get an advance from your publisher any more. They printed three thousand copies of your last book, and two thousand are being remaindered in the drug stores.

Adam: Don't be a snob. I write for the people; and where do you find the people? In the drug stores.

Minerva: Adam Harwick, the great historian. "A lipstick, a tube of toothpaste, and a forty-nine cent biography of Aaron Burr. Will there be anything else, Madame?"

Adam: I should cut you up and put you in that suitcase, limb by limb. But I won't. I'll give you another chance. When I have finished my new book, I hope you'll have the decency to revise your superficial opinion of my work.

Minerva: Sorry, Adam, I'm not waiting for the new book. Which at the rate you've been working, will be finished about 1973. Cockroach!

Adam: I've got him!

Minerva: I've had enough. I'm sick of New York, I'm sick of this apartment, and I think I'm beginning to be sick of you.

Adam: Now Minnie —

Minerva: On second thought, I know I'm sick of you. And if you can bear to hear the absolute truth, I'm tired of supporting you.

Adam: Sure you've supported me! If I had the money, and you didn't have any, I'd support you. And I don't think I'd be so ill mannered as to whine about it.

Minerva: Whine! I've never whined!

Adam: Minnie, stop shouting!

Minerva: And I'm not shouting!

Adam: I'd hate to think that vulgar tone you're now using is your natural voice. *(she slaps him accross the face. he grabs her hair)* You struck me. Remember that — you struck me! Shall I strike her back? *(threatens to strike her with pickle)* No; never! Obviously I must try to reason with her...Now, Minnie, my dear — *(she kicks his shin)* Ouch!

Minerva: Right now I want some peace and some quiet. Some tranquility. A little order in my life, pray God.

Adam: Do you think in Pinneyfield you'll find all that?

Minerva: In Pinneyfield people behave like human beings. They get married, and have children, and go to church on Sundays. And live in clean houses.

Adam: Yes I know; and pay their light bills... But that's not really why you want to go home. Why don't you come right out with it? Your pride is hurt. You got fired from your job last week and you can't take it. You're chicken.

Minerva: There's a train at nine-thirty, I'll just make it.

Adam: I'm surprised at you Minnie. I thought you had guts. What's happened to that girl who was going to set the publishing business on its ear? Who was going to discover tomorrow's Walt Whitman, tomorow's Mark Twain?

Minerva: I'm taking the toenail scissors.

Adam: Sure, let's say you can recognize talent and your boss can't. But did you have to call him a "spineless nincompoop"? Was that exactly diplomatic?

Minerva: But I was right! You know damn well I was right!

Adam: How childish. Even you should know that when you're right is when the boss hates you most. It gives him an inferiority complex. He has to fire you.

Minerva: But he was paying me to tell him the truth.

Adam: Ah, the truth! Haven't you learned by now that nobody wants to be told the truth unless he's already discovered it for himself... And anyway, you've got to abandon this superior attitude. Can't you realize that neither I, nor your boss, nor anyone else in New York gives a hoot in hell that you're the direct descendant of Sarah Pinney? Nevertheless, you're my girl, Minnie, and I love you. Now let's unpack your things — very calmly —

Minerva: Put those things back!

Adam: — then we'll go out to dinner —

Minerva: You know my address. I don't care to hear from you, but if there's any mail, I'd appreciate your fowarding it.

Adam: — I think we'll have a couple of drinks before dinner — and after dinner we'll come back here and —

Minerva: And then you'll make love to me and everything will be just dandy. No, thanks. Definitely, no, thanks.

Adam: Ah, baby — (puts his arms around her)

Minerva: Stay away! Good Lord, the sublime ego of the male who thinks he can cure any woman's unhappiness by going to bed with her.

Adam: An idea occurs to me. Suppose we got married?

Minerva: Married?

Adam: Of course, it wasn't part of our bargain — but I'm perfectly willing — if it would bring into your life any of that tranquility — that serenity —

Minerva: Get out of here! I'm warning you, get out of here!

Adam: Get out of here? I thought you were going!

Minerva: I am!

Adam: And you'll come back. You can't live without me. You'll come back.

Minerva: Not if I live to be eighty and die a spinster!

Adam: Oh, yes you will! You love me!

Minerva: Don't I though! I love you! I love you! I love you!

. . .

Okay, there you are. Now, don't do anything with the scene immediately. Just let it sit in you for a while. Come back tomorrow and continue on to your next assignment.

re-writing
the scene

Before working with the scene in any way, I want you to get some paper and pen. You know what? Why don't you use a little notebook that you can keep together with this book. You will be using it often and it will be helpful to have a place to write down other notes about your work on the scene.

You are now going to re-write the scene without punctuation, without capital letters and without any stage directions. In case you don't know, stage directions are things like: "she kicks his shin." Any of those bits of advice, get rid of 'em. Also, re-write the entire scene, both parts — not just your part.

Here's an example of how it should look:

adam: what in god's name do you think you're doing

minerva: i'm packing don't you have any eyes in your head i'm packing

adam: well you can stop packing stop it right now

minerva: out of my way

adam: you're being rediculous it's late and hotels are expensive

minerva: i'm not going to a hotel i'm going home

Is that clear? Also, I don't want you to use a typewriter or computer to do this, I want you to do this assignment by hand. Please do this now in your notebook and then come back to this book.

. . .

Got that done? Good. From this point on, *you will only work with the scene as you just wrote it.* Now, I want you to read this new version of the scene to yourself. After you do that, come back to the book.

. . .

Okay. Please repond to this question on the space provided here in the book:

Why do you think I had you delete all punctuation, caps and stage directions? How did it feel to read it to yourself in this new format?

_____

_____

_____

_____

_____

_____

_____

. . .

As we talked about earlier, the punctuation makes you think that the lines have to be performed in a certain way. Deleting all this stuff simply makes it easier to break from our preconceived notions of how the scene should go. This scene is chock full of exclamation points and it would be easy to fall into the trap of screaming your way through it. Now, I am not saying that it isn't appropriate to scream if you must. What I am saying is that you must not think it is a requirement of the scene which you must then live up to. Or, just because the script has some little dashes that look like " – " or some periods that look like "..." does that mean you must take a pause at that moment? No, it doesn't.

The same with stage directions. They are either a record of what has happened in previous productions of the play or they are the playwrights ideas about what should happen in a particular moment. But they are not related to the infinite variety of discoveries that will be made as you rehearse the scene. I mean, isn't it possible, if you are playing Minerva, when the moment comes up in which you are told by the stage direction to "kick his shin," that you have the impulse to pinch his nose? It's possible, right? Well, why not give his nose a good pinch? He'll still be able to say his "ouch" line won't he? (And, you guys playing Adam certainly don't have to "threaten to strike her with a pickle." Oh no, you already went out and bought a barrel of pickles?)

By the way, did you wonder why I asked you not to use a computer or typewriter when re-writing the scene? There's something about doing it by hand with a pen or pencil on paper that "plants" the words inside you in some mysterious way. Not only is it good for beginning to get more intimate with the meaning of the scene, it also helps when it becomes time to start learning the words – which is not now! Did you hear that? I do not want you to start learning the words yet. We will get to that later.

Let's move on to your next assignment.

relating it
to the exercise

In your working through my previous two Meisner
books, you learned how to "build" a very specific kind of
improvisational exercise. It had a certain structure to it.
What I want you to do now, in the space provided, is first,
write down what the integral elements of an exercise are.
Just make a list. Then, write down how the scene that I
have just given you compares to the exercise. In other
words, if you imagined that this scene was an exercise
brought into class by two students named Minerva and
Adam, I want you to write down, very simply, how these
two students set up their exercise. Please do that now.

• • •

Let's go over this assignment together now. Going back to the exercise, you may remember that the elements necessary are:

1. One partner is in the room.

2. The partner in the room has an activity that is extremely meaningful to her or him. In the initial stages of the activity, there was a specific physical difficulty. In the preparation work, that difficulty became more of an emotional one. At one point we added urgency to the activity, which was a specific time limit. However it is built, the activity always has to be specific in terms of what it is you're trying to accomplish. (So that WHO knows what it is you must accomplish? So that YOU DO!)

3. The other partner is coming to the door.

4. The person coming to the door has just had something happen – or – has just found something out that is extremely meaningful to her or him. In the early exercises, what you chose could not have anything to do with the partner in the room. Later, we said that what the person coming to the door just had happen or just found out MUST specifically be about or include (in some way) the partner in the room.

5. Finally, there is a specific relationship between the two partners.

So, relating the scene between Minerva and Adam to the exercise, here's what we have:

1. Minerva is in the room with the activity.

2. Minerva's activity is packing her belongings to move back home.

3. Adam is coming to the door.

4. What brings Adam to the door is that he has just found out that his girlfriend Minerva is leaving him.

5. The relationship is girlfriend and boyfriend.

I'm not going to discuss these elements right now, I don't want to speak *yet* about their significance to Minerva and Adam or about the emotional implications of these circumstances. In fact, we are going to leave this scene for a while and come back to it later when we will look in much greater detail at the lives of Minerva Pinney and Adam Harwick. I will also work with you on how you must look at the script as the person who is going to play either of the parts. First, for more practice in relating the scene to the exercise, I am going to give you another scene to read. Here's the scene:

The Old Beginning by Horton Foote
The Characters: Tommy Mavis and H.T. Mavis

Before you read, I want you to know that I have deleted parts of the scene that include other characters and altered some of the lines to create a scene that works well for the purpose of using it as a two person exercise. (Don't worry, Horton told me I could.) Some of my "in person" students have done this scene beautifully. It is always a treat to get to work on anything written by Horton, he's the best there is!

Tommy: Dad, I want you to understand exactly why I was half an hour late.

Mavis: Sit down, son. Sit down. Don't bother me. I'm very busy.

Tommy: Dad, I insist.

Mavis: Sh Tommy sh... *(Tommy starts to speak again. Then he thinks better of it. He goes to a chair. He glares at his father.)*

Tommy: I did it to show you that I cannot be humiliated and intimidated by telephone messages at drug stores and it's going to stop.

Mavis: Oh, I'm not trying to humiliate you. I just know how absentminded you are, that's all.

Tommy: I am not absentminded. I have as much sense of responsibility as you have or anyone else. You and I are going to have a long talk about this once and for all.

Mavis: Just a minute boy, boy. Just a minute. Now about the store I gave you last night. Frankly, son, I gave it to you to teach you a little lesson in humility. To show you how hard it is to earn a dollar of your own. I thought it was the last place in town that would ever rent, but I was fooled. I just finished renting it for you.

Tommy: You rented it?

Mavis: Yes, sir, and got an excellent price, if I do say so myself.

Tommy: Who did you rent it to?

Mavis: Good Deal Stores, Inc. Fine, forward-looking firm. I could have rented them another building, but I decided to give my boy a break.

Tommy: Thank you, Dad, but I'm sorry... *(Mavis hands Tommy some papers.)*

Mavis: Now take these over to the courthouse right away. These are the papers turning the building over to you. I want them filed before I leave.

Tommy: Dad, I'm sorry. But I rented the building this morning.

Mavis: You what?

Tommy: I rented the building this morning.

Mavis: What do you mean renting something without consulting me first? I swear, Tommy. Sometimes I just don't know.

Tommy: But you gave me the building, Dad. The whole point of it was...

Mavis: Naturally I expected to be consulted. You haven't the experience, boy. Have you signed anything yet?

Tommy: No. But I've agreed to it.

Mavis: Who did you rent it to?

Tommy: Lee Johnson. He's moving his secondhand store over there.

Mavis: How much have you agreed to rent it for?

Tommy: Fifty a month.

Mavis: Well, call him up and tell him the whole thing is off.

Tommy: Dad ...

Mavis: Hurry up, son, and call him. I haven't much time. I have a suit to buy. I have gotten you a fine price for the building. A hundred and twenty-five dollars.

Tommy: Dad, I don't want to do it this way.

Mavis: The subject is closed. Tommy, will you please call Lee Johnson?

Tommy: I'm not going to call him, Dad.

Mavis: And why not?

Tommy: Because I don't want to.

Mavis: Very well then, I'll call him myself.

Tommy: And I don't want you calling him either.

Mavis: And why not?

Tommy: Because it's my building. The first thing in my life that ever belonged to me, and I'm going to do with it as I please.

Mavis: *(Sarcastically.)* And what do you please to do with it? Rent it at seventy-five dollars loss a month?

Tommy: I don't know what I'll do yet. But I'm making up my own mind.

Mavis: Look, Tommy...

Tommy: And that's final.

Mavis: Very well. Then I guess I will just have to take my building back.

Tommy: Dad, I beg you not to do this to me...

Mavis: Do what to you?

Tommy: Rent this building over my head.

Mavis: I swear, Tommy, sometimes you talk like a crazy man. Now, let's not talk any more about it or I'm gonna get mad. Here take the check and forget about it...

Tommy: I don't want the check. I don't want the building.

Mavis: Take the check, son.

Tommy: I don't want it. You keep it. I think it's much more important to you.

Mavis: Oh, you do. Well, maybe it is. *(He takes the check.)* Maybe I better keep it. I don't think you're ready for it yet. You know I think the trouble with you, Tommy, is that you've had everything too easy. You've never made a dime of your own. You don't know how hard it is to come by.

Tommy: I think I work pretty hard here.

Mavis: Frankly, you do nothing but get in my way and make things twice as tough as they would be ordinarily.

That's what you do. Now I put up with you, because you're my son, but I'm not gonna have a little two-bit kid that hasn't sense enough to come in out of the rain telling me what to do and what not to do.

Tommy: I'm not trying to tell you what to do or what not to do. I just don't want you to give me something and then tell me...

Mavis: I'll tell you anything I please as long as you're working for me, and you'd better get that straight. Now if you want to do with a thing as you like then go out and get a job and earn your brick building.

Tommy: Now let me tell you what I think of you. I think you're domineering and egotistical and cold-blooded and ruthless. All you care about is getting your own way. From this moment on, I'm through. I wouldn't work for you now if you got down on your knees and begged me to.

Mavis: Don't talk to me like that.

Tommy: You think money can buy anything. Well, it can't buy me. I'm through. *(He walks out of the office.)*

• • •

If you read the play, you'll see that not only did I delete the part of the mother from the scene, I also changed which characters speak a few of the lines. Again, this was to make it work as a two person scene assignment. Now, as you did with the Minerva and Adam scene, I want you to compare the scene with Tommy and Mavis to an exercise:

a) Who is in the room?

_____

_____

b) What is his activity?

_____

_____

c) Who is coming to the door?

_____

_____

d) What is bringing him to the door?

_____

_____

e) What is their relationship?

_____

_____

· · ·

Here are my answers:

a. Mavis is in the room.

b. His activity is working on the contracts for the transfer of ownership of the building Good Deal Stores has rented from him, to his son Tommy.

e. Tommy is coming to the door.

d. He is brought to the door because of an upsetting telephone message from Mavis, which he received at the drug store.

e. The relationship is Father and Son. We also know that Tommy, the Son, works for his Father.

· · ·

Now, before we get back to working on our scene with Minerva and Adam, lets do some exploring of this scene with Tommy and Mavis. As I mentioned earlier, we are looking at the scene out of context of the play. At this stage, I want you to be able to concentrate on the information presented to you by the scene itself without dealing with the greater complexities of the entire play. (Ultimately, of course, you must always read the entire play when working on a scene or a monologue. And, we will get to that in book four.)

You know, when you are at home trying to put together all the elements of an exercise, what you are involved in doing is creating the imaginary circumstances of a dramatic encounter; one with heightened emotional meaning, high stakes and urgency. You are setting the stage for an event in which you don't know what you will be walking into when you enter the room or how the other person is going to respond to you. Or, if you are the person in the room with the activity, these are circumstances in which you know one thing – that you must get this vitally important thing done no matter what. That, in fact, the only way to achieve your own deeply held need is by accomplishing this thing and this thing only, RIGHT NOW!

The scenes I have shown you, contain these elements in various forms. So, let's look at how I came up with my answers when I related the Tommy and Mavis scene to the exercise. And while we're at it, let's also discuss what the real "heart of the matter" is for both of these characters.

First of all, I want you to respond to this question:

If you were playing Tommy, what would the nature of your emotional preparation be before you could come to the door? Also write down how you arrived at your answer.

Please do that now:

_____

_____

_____

_____

_____

_____

_____

Here's my answer:

The actor playing Tommy would have to come to the door out of a preparation that gets him into an emotional place of being fed up! Fed up and determined to put an end to a terrible situation.

How did I arrive at this conclusion? From the scene, we don't know exactly what the message from Mavis to Tommy at the drug store was, but we do know that it is part of an ongoing and upsetting issue between them and which Tommy is now coming home to stop. Again, let's look at the script. Tommy says:

> "Dad, I want you to understand exactly why I was half an hour late. ...I did it to show you that I cannot be humiliated and intimidated by telephone messages at drug stores"

> "And it's going to stop..."

> "You and I are going to have a long talk about this once and for all."

Now wait. Before I continue, I want to highlight something here and make an obvious point even more obvious. How did I just arrive at my conclusions about Tommy? I'll ask that again.

How did I arrive at my conclusions about Tommy?

Stop and think for a moment...

The answer, as you probably guessed, is that I went to the script. This is the crucial point I am offering to you right now. You must understand that —

THE SCRIPT IS YOUR BIBLE.

Everything you need is in the script. If you know how to really look at it, to investigate it, the script will feed you and inspire you. It is very important that, as you make your choices about the scene, you don't conjecture or assume anything. You must always be led to your choices by the information given to you in the script.

Here's my next question:

If you were the actor playing Mavis, what kind of meaning would you want to give to the activity you are involved in at the beginning of the scene? In other words, what kind of emotional preparation would you do to begin the scene and how is it related to the activity? Include how you arrived at your answer.

Please do that now:

_____

_____

_____

_____

_____

_____

_____

_____

Here's my answer:

The actor playing Mavis would need to prepare in such a way that he is in a triumphant state to begin the scene. Then, he can get to work on those papers transferring the title of the building to Tommy.

How did I arrive at this answer? Well, first of all, Mavis just consummated a deal on renting the building out, a building which he considered nearly un-rentable. He also got a good price on it. Look at what Mavis says in the following exchange:

> Mavis: ...I thought it was the last place in town that would ever rent, but I was fooled. I just finished renting it for you.

> Tommy: You rented it?

> Mavis: Yes, sir, and got an excellent price, if I do say so myself.

> Tommy: Who did you rent it to?

> Mavis: Good Deal Stores, Inc. Fine, forward-looking firm. I could have rented them another building, but I decided to give my boy a break.

I also believe that Mavis is excited because he gets to show Tommy who the real pro is around here, and who's the boss. It certainly isn't because he just did a kind and generous thing for his son. Now, why do you think I'd say that? Well first of all, what kind of building did Mavis give to his son? Was it one that he thought would help Tommy have some success so that Tommy could feel a sense of real accomplishment? No! He gave Tommy a building which would make it very difficult for Tommy to succeed. We don't hear Mavis say, "I gave you a building because you work hard and you deserve to feel like an equal part of the firm and because I love you and want to make sure that you feel good about working with me." That's a very different kind of Father, isn't it. What we do hear Mavis say is:

"Now about the store I gave you last night. Frankly, son, I gave it to teach you a little lesson in humility. To show you how hard it is to earn a dollar of your own. I thought it was the last place in town that would ever rent..."

Let me ask you something. Knowing what we just discussed, should I think that Mavis is a terrible man and a mean father? If I am playing Mavis, I must not. I am telling you that you must always look at any character you play in a positive light. Unless you fall in love with the character you are going to play, you cannot play him or her. Every character, no matter what their actions are, has good reasons for doing the things they do. (Isn't that true in life?) It will be your job to discover and understand those good reasons and, to make those good reasons your own!

Okay. Now, as practice, I want you to complete the following:

Write down the things that are of primary importance to Tommy and show specifically how the scene led you to these things. Please do that now:

TOMMY

_____

_____

_____

_____

_____

_____

_____

_____

_____

_____

_____

_____

_____

_____

_____

_____

_____

_____

_____

_____

_____

_____

_____

_____

TOMMY

_____

_____

_____

_____

_____

_____

_____

_____

_____

_____

_____

_____

_____

_____

_____

_____

_____

_____

_____

_____

_____

_____

_____

_____

relating it to the exercise 45

. . .

Here are my responses to the writing assignment:

1. STANDING ON HIS OWN TWO FEET.

Tommy is tired of being treated badly and being considered incompetent by Mavis and he is finally taking steps to stand up to him. What steps? Well first, as Tommy tells Mavis, he purposely comes to the office a half hour late. Then, he defends himself to Mavis, absolutely directly. Tommy says:

> *"I cannot be humiliated and intimidated by telephone messages..."*

> *"I am not absentminded."*

> *"I have as much sense of responsibility as you have..."*

> *"You and I are going to have a long talk about this once and for all."*

2. THE BUILDING.

First we learn that Mavis gave a building to Tommy:

Mavis: Now about the store I gave you last night...

Tommy learns for the first time, in the following exchange, that Mavis has rented this building to someone:

Mavis: ...I just finished renting it for you.

Tommy: You rented it?

Mavis: Yes, sir, and got an excellent price, if I do say so myself.

We find out that Tommy has already rented his building to someone:

Tommy: Dad, I'm sorry. But I rented the building this morning.

We also learn that this building has great importance to Tommy:

Tommy: ...it's my building. The first thing in my life that ever belonged to me, and I'm going to do with it as I please.

Isn't this also part of Tommy's determination to finally stand up to his Dad? Yes it is, as we see here:

Mavis: Well, call him up and tell him the whole thing is off.

Tommy: Dad...

Mavis: Hurry up, son, and call him. I have gotten you a fine price for the building. A hundred and twenty-five dollars.

Tommy: Dad, I don't want to do it this way.

Mavis: The subject is closed. Tommy, will you please call Lee Johnson?

Tommy: I'm not going to call him, Dad.

And finally, Tommy tells Mavis:

Tommy: I don't know what I'll do yet. But I'm making up my own mind... And that's final.

3. HIS RELATIONSHIP WITH MAVIS.

Of course, everything we have just mentioned is directly intertwined with the issue of Tommy's relationship with his Dad, but let's take a closer look. Do you think Tommy feels that his father trusts or appreciates him? I don't think so, listen again to these words:

Tommy: The first thing in my life that ever belonged to me...

Try saying these words to yourself a number of times:

The first thing in my life that ever belonged to me...
The first thing in my life that ever belonged to me...
The first thing in my life that ever belonged to me...
The first thing in my life that ever belonged to me...
The first thing in my life that ever belonged to me...
The first thing in my life that ever belonged to me...
The first thing in my life that ever belonged to me...

The first thing in my life that ever belonged to me...
The first thing in my life that ever belonged to me...
The first thing in my life that ever belonged to me...

Now do it again with your eyes closed for a few minutes...

How did that feel inside to say those words to yourself? Did you get a sense of desperation? Of loneliness and sadness? It's a potent line, don't you think? We also know that, from Tommy's point of view, he is betrayed by his Dad; that in his Father's world, Tommy is clearly less important to Mavis than his business:

Tommy: Dad, I beg you not to do this to me...

Mavis: Do what to you?

Tommy: Rent this building over my head.

Mavis: I swear, Tommy, sometimes you talk like a crazy man. Now, let's not talk any more about it or I'm gonna get mad. Here take the check and forget about it....

Tommy: I don't want the check. I don't want the building.

Mavis: Take the check, son.

Tommy: I don't want it. You keep it. I think it's much more important to you.

Mavis: Oh, you do. Well, maybe it is.

Finally, we also see that Tommy has many pent-up feelings about Mavis which erupt in this line:

> *Tommy: Now let me tell you what I think of you. I*
> *think you're domineering and egotistical and*
> *cold-blooded and ruthless. All you care about is*
> *getting your own way.*

· · ·

As further practice, I want you to do the same kind of exploration for Mavis. This time, you're on your own, as I won't be giving you my own answers.

On the following blank page, write down the important issues to Mavis and how they are justified in the script.

Please do that now:

MAVIS

_____

_____

_____

_____

_____

_____

_____

_____

_____

_____

MAVIS

_____

_____

_____

_____

_____

_____

_____

_____

_____

_____

_____

_____

_____

_____

_____

_____

_____

_____

_____

_____

_____

_____

_____

_____

relating it to the exercise 51

the mechanical reading

We are now going to re-join Minerva and Adam as I show you the first step in working on the scene with your partner. This part of the process, the "mechanical reading," is a great continuation of the kind of "allowing the words to work on you" that you have been doing by reading the scene to yourself without punctuation and stage directions. The main additions are that now you will be doing it together with your acting partner and you will be doing it out loud. (And just to remind you, you will continue to work with the re-written scene, the one without punctuation, etc. As I said earlier, you will no longer use the original scene.)

Before I show you how to do the mechanical reading, I want to talk with you a little about the aim here. Imagine for a moment a painter picking up his brush and then reaching for his palette filled with a variety of beautiful colors. Now imagine the painter, hungry to fulfill a vision burning inside him, actually turning to the big, blank canvas on which he will paint. This is a moment filled with potential, isn't it? And if the painter spends some time here just "being with" the blank canvas and if he doesn't rush, he will be led by the true impulse to put down the first stroke. This is important because once that paint is down on the canvas, it's down there. And in some way, no matter how much he tries to cover it up or mush it around, it will always remain there.

If you have been in plays or worked on scenes in classes, you may have seen a lot of what I am about to describe. Encouraged by directors (or acting teachers) who have no understanding or direct experience of the acting process, many actors do a whole bunch of acting from the very first reading with the other cast members. Why? Basically, it comes down to fear and the desire to look good. The director is afraid that if the actor doesn't give a "great performance" right away, he or she never will. And not knowing how to work with an actor, they fear that they will be put in a position of being asked for guidance and they will be discovered for the fraud they truly are. The actor is afraid to look bad in the eyes of the director and the other actors. Everybody wants to prove to everyone else how wonderful they are. So, from day one, everybody pretends to know it all. Silly, isn't it? The truth is, the actors who give all of their big performances in early rehearsals rarely progress any further and they end up doing on stage what they have planned out in their heads from the first time they read the script. This way of working leaves no room for true discovery of anything. There is certainly no chance for a true relationship with the character they are playing or with the other actors there on stage with them.

What I am advocating is a willingness not to do anything for a while. I am suggesting that you spend some time sitting with all of your beautiful colors and your brush and not put anything down on the canvas right away. And a great way to accomplish this is with the mechanical reading. This is a slow and relaxed reading of the scene — syllable by syllable. I'll say it again. You will read in a relaxed and easy manner,

syllable by syllable.

Since you can't hear me do an example of a mechanical reading, let me write out what I mean. Here are some of the lines from the scene. Try reading them along with me outloud. (Just as practice for a moment, read all of the lines, not just your own.) Nice and easy now, syl-la-ble-by-syl-la-ble:

Adam: what-in-gods-name-do-you-think-youre-do-ing

Minerva: im-pack-ing-dont-you-have-an-y-eyes-in-your-head-im-pack-ing

Adam: well-you-can-stop-pack-ing-stop-it-right-now

Minerva: out-of-my-way

Adam: youre-be-ing-re-dic-u-lous-its-late-and-ho-tels-are-ex-pen-sive

Minerva: im-not-go-ing-to-a-ho-tel-im-go-ing-home

Adam: good-grief-home-to-mo-ther-mi-ner-va-pin-
ney-re-turns-to-ma-ma-and-the-an-ces-tral-
home-stead-you-dis-a-point-me-dar-ling-this-
star-ted-out-as-a-good-ho-nest-row-but-now-
you're-be-ing-co-mon-place

Minerva: im-not-your-dar-ling-and-i-ne-ver-want-
to-see-you-a-gain-and-please-go-in-the-oth-er-
room

Okay, that's a start. Now, you are ready to do the mechanical reading with your scene partner. So:

1. Get your scene partner.

2. Sit at a table directly across from each other.

3. Put your scripts in front of you on the table.

Before I let you start reading, I want to give some pointers about doing the mechanical reading with each other. Why don't you both go over these notes together first and then you'll read. (By the way, it will sound much more complicated than it is. Once you start doing it with each other, it gets very simple.)

Remember, this is the first time the two of you will hear each other saying the words of the characters, so this is an opportunity for the two of you to take some time to get to know each other in a new way. It's also the first time you will be speaking your own words out loud. As you will see, the mechanical reading makes it impossible to do a whole bunch of acting right away.

The way I have always thought of it is in relationship to "meaning." If you are trying to act the part before you are ready, basically, you are trying to slap some kind of meaning on the words which you don't really have yet. (I am saying that you don't *yet* know what you are talking about.) And then, you start spitting all those meaningless words out of your mouth trying futilely to make everyone else believe that you know what you are talking about. But when you make no effort to force meaning on to those words coming out of your mouth, and as you simply speak the words syllable by syllable, and listen to your partner do the same, you are actually allowing your own connection to the circumstances take root and deepen in you – down in your gut.

As you read, do not look at each other. Stay with your script and simply listen to each other. Next, I want you to read without any inflection and at a nice easy volume. Think of it as a steady stream of water flowing at a constant easy pace without any obstructions to that flow. When I say no inflection, think of it as all read on one note. See what note the first syllable comes out of your mouth and if it is comfortable, stay on that note throughout. So, at the end of your lines don't bring your inflection down as if there was a period there and don't bring your inflection up as if there were a question mark. Certainly don't raise your volume as if there were an exclamation point there. When you come to the end of your line, simply stop talking and your partner will continue with her or his line.

Importantly, do not force the syllable by syllable nature of the reading so that you end up sounding like a robot. The syllables should come out of your mouth on a continual flow of air until the air runs out. Then what? Well, take in some more air and keep going. I am saying that you should not treat each syllable like it is its own sentence. So, no "glottal attack" or glottal stopping. (Glottal attack is the sound made by a momentary complete closure of the glottis, followed by an explosive release. What the hell's a glottis? It's actually the space between the vocal cords at the upper part of your larynx.)

All right. So you are at the table across from your partner and you have your scripts on the table in front of you.

4. Look at each other for a moment and just "be" with each other.

5. Then, both of you look down at your scripts.

6. Now begin and complete a mechanical reading of your scene.

• • •

How did that feel? Remember, nice and easy. Now, I want you to do at least three more mechanical readings with your partner before moving on to your next assignment. Do not do more than one reading together per day. So, I'll see you back here in a few days. Have fun.

the working reading

Now we move on to the next stage of working with your partner on the scene and it's called a "working reading." We are no longer reading the scene syllable by syllable — that phase of the work is finished.

First I will give you instructions, then I want you both to do a working reading. Here's the way it works:

1. Once again, sit at the table directly across from your partner.

2. Have your scripts in front of you. (For this reading, it is a good idea to hold the script in one hand and with the other hand, keep a finger running along with the words you are reading so that when you need to, you can

easily find the place where you left off. You'll see what I mean.)

3. Without saying anything, get in contact with your partner. Just be with each other for a few moments.

4. Whoever has the first line will go down to the script and get some words. You get as many as you can remember. Then, look back at your partner and, with those words, talk to your partner. Go back and get some more words and, once again, look back at your partner and talk to your partner. Do this until you have spoken the entire line.

5. Then the other person goes down to the script, gets some words, looks back at the partner and speaks.

6. Continue through the entire scene in this manner.

Before you begin the working reading, I want to give you some guidelines.

First of all, the whole point of the working reading is to "really talk / really listen." I'll say that again.

The whole point of the working reading is to "really talk / really listen."

I am saying that now, you must begin to really talk to your partner and you must really listen to him or her. This means, starting to "work off" each other — which requires that you are available and in response to each other.

In working off of each other, allow whatever happens to happen. Do not censor any of your responses because you think they are not "appropriate" to what is happening in the scene. You mustn't worry about that. Of course, at the same time, you mustn't force anything to happen. You must simply give yourself the freedom to see where the scene takes you as you work off of your partner.

Do not rush this reading. Take your time. "Pace" is the last thing in the world that should be on your mind.

Do not talk into your script. What I mean is, you should not be looking at your script when you are speaking. Remember, your fuel on stage is your partner, not those pieces of paper. So, get the words and before you say a thing, get back in contact with your partner and really talk to her or him.

It is also very important that the partner who is not speaking stay in contact with the partner who is talking. I am saying that when your partner is talking, you must not be looking down into your script preparing to get your next line. When you do that, you are no longer really listening, are you? And remember, I said that this reading is all about "really talk / really listen!" How will you know when it is your turn to speak? Well, if you are really listening, you will know when your partner is done talking and that it is time for you to go get some words.

Don't worry about remembering the entire line. As I said, get as many words as you can and then talk to your partner. When you run out of words, go back down and get some more words. This is where having your finger on the place where you left off is so helpful. The more you do this kind of reading, the easier this way of working will become – you will become more adept at getting those words off of the page and getting right back with your partner.

Is all of that clear? It's time now to do a working reading. (Actually, I want you to do a total of five working readings. Do one a day.) After you have done your *first* working reading with your partner, and only after you have done it, please continue in the book.

A s s i g n m e n t   S i x

exploring
the scene

Since you are reading these words (for those of you actually working on the scene,) you are telling me that you have completed your first of five working readings with your partner. It is now time to take a closer look at the circumstances of the scene and their meaning to Minerva and Adam. First, I want you to know that the reason I have given you this particular scene as a jumping off place for working with text is because it isn't complicated and it is clearly structured like an exercise. The circumstances are simple and unambiguous and I think most of you can relate to them in some way. Later, we will take a look at some scenes that are more complex and rich. So, right now, let's review how we related this scene to an exercise:

1. Minerva is in the room with the activity.

2. Minerva's activity is packing her belongings to move back home.

3. Adam is coming to the door.

4. What brings Adam to the door is that, in the middle of an argument with his girlfriend Minerva, he has just found out that she is leaving him.

5. The relationship is girlfriend and boyfriend.

Next, on the following blank pages, I want you to:

Write down the things that are of primary importance to the character you are playing and show specifically how the scene led you to these things. Please do that now:

MINERVA

_____

_____

_____

_____

_____

_____

_____

_____

_____

MINERVA

_____

_____

_____

_____

_____

_____

_____

_____

_____

_____

_____

_____

_____

_____

_____

_____

_____

_____

_____

_____

_____

_____

ADAM

_____

_____

_____

_____

_____

_____

_____

_____

_____

_____

_____

_____

_____

_____

_____

_____

_____

_____

_____

_____

_____

_____

_____

_____

Let's take a look at the scene together. First, we'll talk about Minerva. Here are Minnie's key circumstances and how she feels about them:

1. MINERVA'S RELATIONSHIP WITH ADAM.

We know that Minerva is absolutely fed up and disgusted with Adam. She's had it with his laziness, with how untrustworthy and undependable he is, and she is sick of carrying the weight of supporting him financially. Here are some of the things she says to Adam:

"i'm not your darling and I never want to see you again"

"adam why didn't you pay the light bill i gave you the money"

"but you spent the money"

"you can't even get an advance from your publisher anymore"

"i'm not waiting for the new book which at the rate you've been working will be finished about 1973"

"i know i'm sick of you"

"i'm tired of supporting you"

2. MINERVA AND HER LIFE IN NEW YORK.

Minnie is also fed up with the kind of life she has been living in New York and longs for a more reliable and stable way of life. She wants the kind of life she believes people have in her home town Pinneyfield. She says:

"cockroach"

"i'm sick of new york"

"i'm sick of this apartment"

"right now i want some peace and some quiet some tranquility a little order in my life pray god"

"in pinneyfield people behave like human beings they get married and have children and go to church on sundays and live in clean houses"

As you noticed, I included Minnie noticing the cockroach. Don't you think that her seeing it in the middle of packing adds to her sense of repulsion towards her life here? I would also include in this talk about "life in New York," Minnie's job. We know that she worked in publishing and that she's been fired for criticizing her boss. Here's the exchange that tells us:

> *Adam: ...what happened to that girl who was going to set the publishing business on its ear who was going to discover tomorrows walt whitman tomorrows mark twain*
>
> *Minnie: i'm taking the toenail scissors*

Adam: sure let's say you can recognize talent and your boss can't but did you have to call him a spineless nincompoop was that exactly diplomatic

Minnie: but i was right you know damn well i was right

Adam: how childish even you should know that when you're right is when the boss hates you most it gives him an inferiority complex he has to fire you

Minnie: but he was paying me to tell him the truth

Okay, let's talk about the circumstances for Adam:

1. ADAM'S RELATIONSHIP WITH MINERVA.

All I will say, right now, about Adam's relationship with Minerva's is that when he discovers she is leaving him, he expresses very clearly that he doesn't want her to go. (I'll talk more specifically about Adam's point of view towards Minnie in a little while.) When Adam comes in and finds Minerva packing, he says:

"well you can stop packing stop it right now"

Later he says:

"nevertheless you're my girl minnie and i love you now let's unpack your things very calmly"

2. ADAM THE AUTHOR.

We learn that Adam is an author and that he is working on a new book. Here's the information we get from Adam:

"if i find ten dollars in my pocket and i need books i buy the books"

"i write for the people"

"when i have finished my new book i hope you'll have the decency to revise your superficial opinion of my work"

We also get some information from Minerva:

"adam harwick the great historian a lipstick a tube of toothpaste and a forty nine cent biography of aaron burr will there be anything else madame"

Well, those are the basic issues of importance to each of the characters. As I said earlier, this is not a complicated scene — so — let's not complicate it. Now, before continuing in this section, I want you and your partner to do the second of your working readings. When you have done that, come back to this point in the book. Take your time, I'm gonna go watch my DVD copy of "Shine."

. . .

You're back? How did your working reading go? To continue exploring the scene, which really means investigating the circumstances of the scene from various angles, I am going to introduce you to two invented students who, like you, are working on the scene. Their names are Darby and Marvin.

Darby and Marvin are in class and have just completed their second working reading. Here's my invented conversation with them:

Larry: Okay, let's talk about the scene. Darby, talk to me about what's going on here for you.

Darby: Well, she is very upset about her...

Larry: Darby.

Darby: Yes.

Larry: At this point it would be good to talk in terms of "I." It's you playing the part, right?

Darby: Yes, right.

Larry: So, tell me about what's going on here.

Darby: I have to get out of New York and away from this creep because my life is going down the tubes here.

Larry: What does that mean to you, going down the tubes.

Darby: I'm wasting my life away. I have a boss who is an idiot and doesn't value my opinion and I have a jerk for a boyfriend who I can't trust. So I just quit my stupid job and I am ending things with Adam.

Larry: Tell me more about your relationship with Adam.

Darby: I have been wasting my time with him. He is a lousy writer and he has no income. I have to support him financially and now, I find out that the money I give him to pay the bills with, he goes out and throws away on books. He's not even sorry about it. He's an arrogant son-of-a-bitch and he thinks that I'm just going to put up with his bullshit. So I am leaving him.

Larry: What about Pinneyfield?

Darby: That's where I grew up and that's where people lead lives with strong family values and security and I want that. I want children and I want to make a nice home for my family and I want a man to love me and treat me with respect and I want to go to church and have a relationship with God and my life here feels very Godless. It's like being in New York is a dead end track I'm on.

Larry: I can see that has some meaning for you doesn't it. It has meaning for you, Darby.

Darby: Yes, it does.

Larry: Would you be willing to talk about that?

Darby: Yes. Sometimes I feel that my life is very empty and that I often turn to my boyfriend to fill it up but he can't. I have a job that really doesn't nourish me in any way except to pay the bills and I'm feeling pretty depressed because it's like that's what my life is about right now — going to work, coming home, cooking and paying the bills, going to sleep and getting up and going back to work again. Most of my life is... (She stops talking for a moment and puts her head down and sighs. Some tears fall to the table onto her script. She wipes her eyes with the back of her right hand. Darby continues very quietly.) Most of my life is being eaten up doing something that I could care less about. Yuchhhh, I hate it! I want so much more. I just feel like I'm stuck on the wrong track.

Larry: That's what you said about Minnie.

Darby: Hmmm?

Larry: You said that Minnie is on a dead end track.

Darby: Yes.

Larry: You've found a strong connection to what Minerva is going through.

Darby: Yes. It's funny, when I first read the scene, I was afraid that it was just this big shouting match and there was nothing here but a bunch of anger. I didn't even realize until talking just now, how much pain is really underneath all that anger for me, you know, I mean for Minnie... well, I'm using "I" now, so... I mean for me. Yeah, I can really relate to what's going on here.

Larry: Thanks Darby, I'm going to talk with Marvin now. Marvin, tell me about the circumstances for you.

Marvin: Well, I am pissed off because the girl I love is leaving me and moving back home and I don't want to lose her. I think that's really the main thing here.

Larry: I can only agree with part of what you said Marvin. Yes, absolutely, you don't want to lose her. The part I disagree with is that you love her. Let's look at the scene together and I'll show you why I say that. First of all, what is your profession.

Marvin: I'm a writer.

Larry: What kind of writer are you.

Marvin: Not a good one. I have no income and my publishers won't give me an advance. My last book...

Larry: *(Larry breaks in.)* Marvin.

Marvin: Yes.

Larry: You have to act your part. Let Darby act her part and you act your part. Do you understand?

Marvin: Well... I'm not sure.

Larry: I am saying that you have to act your part; you must work from your point of view, not from hers. Why in the world would you say that you are not a good writer?

Marvin: I can't even get an advance from....

Larry: Wait. Are you a published writer?

Marvin: Yes. I am.

Larry: That's a great thing isn't it? To be a published author?

Marvin: Yes, it is.

Larry: And your published book, is it a trashy novel?

Marvin: No, it's a biography of Aaron Burr.

Larry: So, what kind of writer are you?

Marvin: I guess I am a historian, that's what Minnie calls me.

Larry: And do you write for your own personal gain?

Marvin: What do you mean?

Larry: Who do you write for? It's in the scene. You say...

Marvin: Oh yes, that's right. I say that I write for the people.

Larry: Now Marvin, doesn't that statement give you the feeling that you are involved in something of tremendous importance, something of significance! "I write for the people!"

Marvin: Yes, it does.

Larry: And, in terms of your writing, what are you involved in right now?

Marvin: I am working on my next book.

Larry: What kind of book is it?

Marvin: Well, the scene doesn't say.

Larry: No, not specifically. But the scene does tell us something about it.

Marvin: There's really only two lines about it. When Minnie is putting me down and sarcastically calling me a "great historian," I tell her that I hope she will have the decency to change her opinion of me when I have finished the book I am working on.

Larry: And what's the other line?

Marvin: Minnie talks about how long it's taking me to write the book.

Larry: So, how do these two thing add up. First, you believe she will change her opinion of you when she reads this new book you are writing. Does that make you feel like this is just some old crummy book you are writing or an important one?

Marvin: An important one.

Larry: Right! If you are a writer and you are taking all this time working on your new book, investing your life into it, even using any money that you can get your hands on to buy books that you need — at the expense of pedestrian obligations like paying the bills — do you intend for it to be third rate?

Marvin: No.

Larry: NO! It's going to be your breakthrough work! It's going to be a masterpiece!

Marvin: So, you're saying make it extreme for me, like in the exercise.

Larry: Well look, the text is our jumping-off place, it's our inspiration. We must begin with the text and then allow it to incite our imagination. And remember, we are exploring Adam's point of view right now and then asking what does that mean to you. Let me leave the author part and go back to what you originally mentioned, that you are angry about Minnie leaving and that you love her. I told you that I agreed with the part about not wanting Minnie to leave. Why do you think you'd be angry that Minnie is leaving right now.

Marvin: Well, I really did think it was because I love her. I say it in the scene. I say, "You're my girl, Minnie, and I love you."

Larry: Sometimes we say things to people that we don't really mean and we do it to acheive a certain result, to manipulate that person. Isn't that true?

Marvin: So, you're saying that Adam really doesn't love Minnie.

Larry: Is there anything in the scene that leads you to the idea or the feeling that this guy really cares about this woman? Take a look at the things you say and do in the scene. Here's your girlfriend Minnie who has just lost her job and is very upset about her life. Do you treat her with compassion and understanding?

Marvin: No, I call her commonplace.

Larry: That's right. When she cries, do you put your arm around her and try to comfort her?

Marvin: No, basically, I tell her that her tears won't have any affect on me and that they only make her look messy.

Larry : What other kinds of things do you say to her.

Marvin: Well, I call her lots of names.

Larry: Like what?

Marvin: I call her a snob. I tell her that she is a chicken and that she is childish. I criticize her for having a superior attitude. I even tell her that I should cut her up and put her in the suitcase limb by limb.

Larry: And when she is finally leaving, what do you say to her?

Marvin: I tell her that she will come back because she loves me and she can't live without me.

Larry: Right. You don't say that you love her. You warn her that she won't be able to live without you because she loves you. Now, I know that in the heat of an argument, we say all kinds of things we later regret. But, when you add up all those things that you just told me, do you get the feeling that anywhere in this guy's insides, he really has a true affection and love for Minnie.

Marvin: No, I guess I don't.

Larry: Then why do you think you are so upset that she is leaving?

Marvin: I'm not sure.

Larry: What is the most important thing that you are involved in right now.

Marvin: Working on my new book?

Larry: Yes, that's right. YOUR MASTERPIECE! And while your complete attention must be on your writing, do you have a moment to spare to concern yourself with mundane things like supporting yourself?

Marvin: No, I don't have time for that. I have to write.

Larry: Yes, you have to write. And who makes it possible for you to put all of your energies into your book.

Marvin: Minnie does.

Larry: So why don't you want Minnie to leave?

Marvin: Because if she goes, I lose my total freedom do my work.

Larry: Shit, you'll have to go get a job! You see Marvin? It's not about love, it's about losing your meal ticket. That's especially bad RIGHT NOW because you're on the brink of the most explosive and life altering achievement imaginable! Right?

Marvin: *(He screams.)* That's Right!! *(The class laughs.)*

Larry: Good. Now, for your next working reading, I want both of you to begin with an emotional preparation. (Note: The emotional preparation work is the focus of my *Meisner Approach Workbook Two: Emotional Freedom*.) So, you will go out and prepare first and then you will come in, sit down and do the working reading out of that preparation. Is that clear?

Darby: I have a question.

Larry: Yes, Darby.

Darby: When I prepare, do I prepare from the things that have happened to Minerva?

Larry: That's a good question. Let me ask this. When you come into the room and start packing, whose hands are picking up the clothes and putting them in the suitcase?

Darby: They are my hands.

Larry: And whose voice do we hear demanding to know why Adam didn't pay the light bill?

Darby: It's my voice.

Larry: What am I saying?

Darby: You're saying it's me up there, not some character named Minerva.

Larry: Yes. I am saying that the character is always you. The meaning must come from you. And the more you work on the scene, hopefully, the more you and the point of view of that character are coming together, are meshing in a most wonderfully mysterious way. You see, "character" is really a specific point of view. But we'll talk more about that when we get into the interpretation work (Workbook Four.) So, in terms of the preparation, well... let's review emotional preparation for a moment. *(Larry turns to the class.)* Tell me the important ingredients in emotional preparation.

(The class sits quietly for a moment. Then, Joshua raises his hand.)

Joshua: Well, it's for the first moment only and then you don't know what's going to happen.

Larry: That's right. Preparation is for the first moment. It's what gets you into the room. And once you get there, what do you do with the preparation?

Mandi: You drop it.

Larry: Say a little more Mandi. Explain what you mean by "drop it."

Mandi: What I mean is that the preparation puts you into an emotional state. The fantasizing or whatever else you are doing to prepare outside the room must be left alone once you get to the door and then you work off of your partner.

Larry: Good. What happens if you try in any way to hold onto your preparation?

Tess: It makes it impossible to be present to what your partner is giving to you; to be present to what is really happening.

Larry: That's right on! If you, in any way, try to hold onto the preparation because you you don't think you are emotional enough, where is your attention?

Sarah: It's on yourself.

Larry: Right, your attention is on yourself and what you are doing is no longer related to acting.

Teri: Another important thing was that what we prepare from must be something that has just happened or something that we just found out that is extremely meaningful to us. And, you told us that the word "just" was essential; that it has JUST happened or we have JUST found it out.

Larry: Hey, Teri, you take great notes! Yes, the word "just" is essential. And remember, as with the activities, the reasons you work with in the preparation must always be based on an element of truth. What is the element of truth?

Tess: The element of truth is its true importance to me. I start with the element of truth and then take it into the land of my imagination. I took good notes too! *(The class laughs again.)*

Larry: Yes, that's right, into the land of your imagination! Now, back when I introduced you to preparation, I also told you how the preparation relates to the text. Do you remember?

Carol: You said that the nature of the preparation is determined by the circumstances of the scene and what has happened to the character just before the scene begins.

Larry: That's it exactly. If your partner's first line to you is, "I've never seen you so excited!" obviously, you better prepare in such a way that when you enter, you are feeling absolutely euphoric! So, yes, where we have to be emotionally in that first moment, is determined by the circumstances of the scene. And, getting back to Darby's question, how does she handle preparing for that first moment when she must come in so upset that she is going to pack, leave her boyfriend and change her life once and for all.

Carol: Like when Darby was talking to you before about the scene, she would have to relate the circumstances to herself and then find a way to prepare personally in such a way that she, Darby, would be that upset.

Larry: So, you are saying that rather than using Minerva's circumstances from the play, she would have to create her own circumstances for the preparation that would get her into that emotional state.

Carol: That's what I think she'd have to do. I mean, the circumstances of the play don't really have a specific personal meaning to her. Like, take Adam, Darby doesn't really have a boyfriend named Adam who's a scum-ball-parasite.

Larry: I'll have to remember that, "scum-ball-parasite!" And, you're right, the scene may have meaning to Darby in all kinds of ways but they are not specifically tied to her own life. YET! You see, the word "specifically" is very important here. As we saw when Darby talked about the scene, she has some strong personal connections to what Minerva is going through. Still, it is important for Darby, in preparing, to make very specific what has just happened to Darby that comes from Darby's life. It may even be very close to the play, but it must come from Darby and her own life (the element of truth) — AND — from her own fertile imagination.

So, in the preparation, she gets to create SPECIFICALLY where she has JUST come from or SPECIFICALLY what she has JUST found out that makes her so upset. Then, she comes to the door and leaves the preparation alone while "riding on" the wave of emotion, the wave of "LIFE" the preparation has induced in her — AND THEN — she turns herself over to her partner; working off what she gets from her partner and from everything in her environment.

Ultimately, the people in the audience are hearing the words and, at one level, are relating to the words in relationship to the story they tell. When you do the real work, the kind of work we are striving for here, you have an impact on the audience at a deeper level. You do this by the meaning you bring to everything you say and everything you do not say! This is how we start to reach an audience where they "live," you know, reach not only their minds but their hearts and their guts. This is the difference between most performances, where the actor is merely spitting out a bunch of empty words and the rare performances, where the actor has infused the words with his or her own life. Remember, I told you that in this work there is a price to pay, there is a cost.

Tom: Larry, what do you mean there is a cost?

Larry: There is a cost and the cost is personal. You know Tom, clearly, this work is not for everyone. Not everyone is interested in it. Not everyone is willing to do what it takes to bring an authentic and human expression to the role. It certainly isn't a comfortable thing to do with your life, so why do it. It's much easier to just "make it look like" something is happening there on stage, to fake and pretend. It's a lot easier and very, very safe. All I know is that the actors who are turned on by the kind of work we are grappling with here in class do it because they have no choice. It's not that they would rather work this way, it's that they must! Here's what I want to do now. Let's take a ten minute break and when we come back, I'll continue with Darby and Marvin and we'll talk about their emotionalpreparations for the scene.

(The class breaks. A few students run for the bathrooms. Some walk out the front door and head down to First Avenue to get some coffee. The others hang out in the lobby of the theatre talking and eating snacks. Larry, his lower back in some pain, stands up and stretches his arms to the ceiling. He picks up his cup of orange juice and soda-water from under his seat, takes a sip and walks into the lobby. Rachel comes over to Larry and asks if they can talk for a moment. This is their conversation:)

Rachel: Larry, I am having a really big problem. *(She starts to cry.)*

Larry: Let's go into the office and talk. *(They walk down the three grey steps at the back of the lobby which lead to the theatre office, dressing rooms and rehearsal hall. Larry walks into the office and takes some scripts off of a chair.)* Rachel, have a seat. *(Rachel sits, blowing her nose into a tissue she had in her pocket. Larry spins the brown desk chair around and sits across from Rachel and waits.)*

Rachel: This work is so important to me Larry, I'll do anything it takes to learn something here. I am having a really big problem with Kevin, my scene partner. He keeps canceling rehearsals and giving me lame excuses. One time he just didn't show up and he didn't call or anything. The next day he told me that he just "zoned out" on the rehearsal. I've tried to accomodate his schedule in every way but that doesn't help. I am really so fucking pissed off at him and he's wasting my time and we've got our open class coming up and I want this scene to be really great and I just want to scream at him.

Larry: Have you told him any of this?

Rachel: Well...not this directly...no, I really haven't told him.

Larry: I think it's very important when your acting partner is screwing you around that you tell him or her exactly how you feel about it. You mustn't put up with it. Also, I want you to tell me as soon as it happens. Please don't wait this long and try to hold it all together on your own. I need to know this stuff is going on right away.

Wait here, I'll be right back. *(Larry goes into the lobby and looks around and then he goes out the front door. He spots Kevin smoking a cigar and goes over to him.)* Kevin, I need to see you in my office.

Kevin: Yeah, sure, as soon as I finish having a smoke.

Larry: No, I need to see you right now. *(Larry turns and walks back in.)*

Kevin: Yeah, sure. *(Kevin takes another puff and blows smoke towards the door. He puts the cigar out on the cement wall and mumbles under his breath. Then Kevin heads inside and back to the office where Larry has cleared another chair.)*

Larry: Have a seat.

Kevin *(Kevin looks over at Rachel. She's looking at the floor.)* All right. *(He sits.)*

Larry: What's the problem with working on your scene Kevin?

Kevin: We have been working on the scene.

Larry: Look Kevin, Rachel needs a partner who is as committed as she is to work on the scene. I think she deserves that. Rachel just told me that you are cancelling rehearsals and not meeting very often to work with her.

Kevin: Hey Larry, we've been working on the scene. Maybe not as much as you've suggested to us in class but—

Larry: No, not suggested, required. I told you all that you are required to meet once a day and put in some work on the scene. I said that for the next few weeks you would have to be unreasonable with yourself in making it happen.

Kevin: Hey, I work ten to five during the week and my work comes first. I'm doing what I can do.

Larry: You are doing what you are willing to do.

Kevin: I am doing what I am able to do.

Larry: What about meeting before work. Can you do that Rachel?

Rachel: I will meet anytime to work on the scene. It's my priority.

Larry: Is there a problem with that Kevin, meeting before work?

Kevin: I don't always know where I will be before I go to work.

Larry: And after work?

Kevin: We are meeting after work.

Rachel: Once a week isn't enough Kevin.

Kevin: I can't give every day after work to this, I have other things going on in my life, too.

Larry: I'm not interested in your story or your excuses Kevin. You simply refuse to get straight with me here, you know that? Kevin, we had this kind of talk when we were doing the exercises and you said you understood what was required here but now the same thing is coming up again. You are simply unwilling to make this work and Rachel is suffering because of it. So, I'm pulling you out of the scene. You can observe the classes on scenework or not, it's up to you. *(Larry stands.)*

Kevin: That's it?

Larry: That's it. It's time to start class. *(Kevin stands and walks out. Rachel stands.)*

Larry: Rachel, I'll get you a new partner right now.

Rachel: Thanks Larry. *(She walks out of the office and heads back to the theatre. Larry follows, locking the door behind him.)*

(Larry has called the class back in from the break. He notices that Kevin has not returned to class and that his belongings are not in his seat. Larry stands in front of the group.)

Larry: I need a scene partner for Rachel. Is anyone interested in working on another scene in addition to their own?

Pete: *(Jumping to his feet.)* I will.

Larry: Are you sure you have the time to work with your partner and with Rachel?

Pete: Yeah, I'm on a three week break from the restaurant and I have plenty of time. I'd love to work on the scene with Rachel.

Larry: Good. Rachel, after class, work out some meetings with Pete and get right to work.

Rachel: I will. Thank you.

Larry : Alright, back to work. Darby and Marvin, come back up and let's finish talking about the emotional preparations for your scene.

(Marvin and Darby come back and sit at the table in front of the class)

Larry: Just to be clear, I want each of you to tell me the nature of your emotional preparation which will bring you to the door.

Darby: I know I have to come in extremely hurt and upset. For me, being in the midst of some awful circumstances in life, and then being betrayed by the person I was counting on most, is what really gets me in this scene. That's what I will prepare from — being betrayed by someone very close to me.

Larry: Being betrayed by Adam?

Darby: Well, after what you have talked about before, no. I will have to prepare from my own imaginary circumstances built around the fact that I have been betrayed by someone who has true meaning to me in my own life.

Larry: That's right, the element of truth! Very good. How about you Marvin?

Marvin: I can relate to what you were talking about before the break, that I am on the verge of a major breakthrough, a major accomplishment. Now, it is being threatened by her leaving. So I am going to prepare from the idea that my imminent success is being sabotaged by her.

Larry: By her?

Marvin: Well, as Darby said, by someone who has real meaning to me.

Larry: Right. *(Larry turns to the class.)* Okay everyone, get to work on these things and for your next working reading, your third working reading,

you will begin with a full preparation.

So, you prepare outside and then you come in and sit at the table and work off of each other.

Before I let you all go, I wanted to mention a film I want you all to see before next class. Many of you may have already seen it, if so, see it again. You can rent the tape. The film is "Jerry Maguire." The reason I want you all to see it is because there is a glowing performance in this film by an actor named Cuba Gooding Jr. that is simply breathtaking. He brings a rich and beautiful life to the part and, everything he does — *everything* — is filled with tremendous meaning and urgency. Everything we are working towards here, he does. And, with great simplicity. You know I can try to describe what he does in many ways, but nothing I can say is good enough to truly reflect the experience of watching him work in this film. I had to watch the film two more times and each time, I have enjoyed him more. It's an inspiration to see this kind of work and it's very important to keep nourishing yourselves in this way. Okay, class dismissed.

(The students begin to pick up their belongings. Many meet their partners out in the lobby to schedule rehearsals. Larry remains in the theatre. Finally, all the students have gone and Larry turns back to his "reader students" who are working their way through his Meisner Book Part Three. Hey! That's you!)

. . .

You're still here? Great! It's time to assign you the third working reading as well. The nature of the preparations should be clear to you and I want you to get ready to work with your partner. So, your third working reading will go as follows:

1. Both partners leave their scripts on the table and go out of the room to prepare.

2. When you are fully prepared, come into the room and sit down. If you are the first one to come into the room, sit at the table and continue your preparation until your partner enters.

3. Once you are both at the table, leave the preparation alone and begin the working reading. Again, when I say to "leave the preparation

alone," I am saying that you must stop the fantasizing or free associating about your imaginary circumstances and you must now give your complete attention to your partner. In this way, you can allow yourself to "ride" fully on what the preparation has induced in you and to work off of what you are getting from your partner in each moment.

4. Have Fun!

learning
the words

Before we get to the next working reading, I want you to begin learning the words of the scene.

Now, the truth is, with all the work you have been doing on the scene, you have already become very familiar with the words. At the same time, you must see that it's not enough to be merely familiar with the words. You must have those words rooted in you so deeply that no matter what happens, they are continually ready to pop out of your mouth without you having to think about them. You will find that, if you do not have this complete a hold on the words, when the scene comes to life on you, the first thing to go will be the words. What I mean is that if you do not really know the words, when suddenly, the scene ignites and you and your partner enter that wonderful and surprising space of unchartered territory which cannot be planned, you will forget the words and — BOOM — all that beautiful life will crash to a halt because you will go right into your head and try to remember what to say next!

Well, what if you do forget the words. How do you handle that? *("Hey! I thought this section was about learning the words not forgetting them?")* Here are a few suggestions which fit into that "easier said than done" category but with practice will be very valuable to you.

I'll start with the most intangible. It's an important phrase to consider in relationship to everything we are dealing with together. Maybe the most important. The phrase is:

to embrace

Let's go to the dictionary.

> embrace: To include, to take up willingly or eagerly, eager acceptance.

I love that, "to take up willingly or eagerly." You see, what you must start to understand is that once you are on stage, there are no mistakes. Have I told you this before? If so, it's worth saying again. Once you are on stage with your partners, *there are no mistakes!*

The only one who can decide that something is a mistake is you. And, if you are able and willing to include everything that happens and make it all okay, then it is. The audience certainly has no expectation that you do or say or feel anything in any particular way.

You know, in live theatre, all kinds of things are bound to happen. Your acting partners will forget lines, doors will fall off their hinges, props won't be where they are supposed to be, you'll trip and split your pants, etc, etc...You better be agile and relaxed and ready to deal with all of it. Of course, this demands that you are willing to EMBRACE all of it rather than denying it. Here's a great example from an interview that appears in my book *The Actor's Guide To Qualified Acting Coaches*. The teacher talking is Phil Gushee, a wonderful acting coach who teaches in New York and who was trained by Sanford Meisner:

> *The second stage of the exercise, working with the independent activities, is about the training in the reality of doing. Of all the things that Sandy said, the one that I made a huge poster of and put up on my wall is, "That which hinders your task is your task." I love that statement, because that's only possible if you're not in your head. I remember in the middle of a production, an actor trained by Bill Alderson was doing a very emotional scene with a woman and the top button of her blouse popped off and rolled to the front of the stage. This guy, without missing a beat, walked down, picked up the button, brought it back, grabbed her hand, put it in her hand and closed her hand over it, all the while continuing the scene. And when it was over, the actress asked him, "How on earth did you ever learn to do that? It happened so suddenly and so spontaneously and you adjusted completely, but yet we continued. The scene, if anything, was enriched and was better." He said to her, "Well, it took me one year of doing Meisner work just to see the button and see it pop off and see where it went*

and see it roll down there and stop at the front of the stage. It took me a second year to trust that I could just go over, reach down, pick it up and bring it back and give it to you. And it took me a third year to learn how to structure a part, and within that, to have the freedom to improvise."

The point I am trying to make is that the worst possible thing to do if you forget your lines is to freak out and try to remember them. The "freaking out" will make it even more difficult to remember the words and it will take you and the audience out of the play. If you first accept what is happening and then continue to work off of your partner, even throwing in some repetition, you will be brought back to the words very naturally. And, I promise you, no one out there watching will even know you lost the words.

That's right, I said use the repetition as a vehicle back to the words of the play. Because, as you know, the repetition keeps you in moment-to-moment contact with your partner and with what is actually happening. By staying with what is happening, what you say and do will be appropriate to the moment and will make sense to the audience. And, it will ultimately lead you to something which will trigger the words from the script. If you are lucky enough to have a partner who is nimble enough to stay with you, you'll both even have some fun. In this way, what would cripple most actors, will just be more great fuel for your acting engine!

Okay, let's move on to learning the words. Some of you may have worked on scenes before and you already have ways of learning the words that work for you. For some of you, this may be the first time that you are working with text. I am going to give you a way of learning the words that I want all of you to try. And, since some of you may have difficulty learning words, I'll also give you a few simple suggestions of some things that may help you learn the words more effectively.

LEARNING THE WORDS BY ROTE

Have you heard that phrase before, to "learn by rote"? It means to learn the words without meaning. Why do you think I would ask you to learn the words without meaning? It is so that, once again, you do not lock yourself into a particular way of saying the words.

You know, Sandy had the most wonderful analogy for what we are working towards right now. He said the words must be like an empty canoe on a river. It is the movement and flow of the river which will determine how the canoe travels on it. If the river becomes still, the canoe will slow to a halt. If the river becomes turbulent, the canoe will bounce around violently. If there is a bend in the river, the canoe will hit the bank and veer off in a new direction. So, again, Sandy said that the words are like the canoe. He also said that the river is what is happening between you and your partner. Do you get that? Like the empty canoe, you must allow the words of the scene to ride freely on the river of life that comes from you and your partner working off of each other. Actually, that river of life will be coming from three things; it comes from what you get from *your partner* in each moment, from how what you get from your partner *affects you,* and from what it is you are *trying to accomplish* (what you are "doing" and why you are doing it!).

Remember, very early on, I told you that acting is doing and when you are not involved in doing something on stage, you are no longer acting. The activities were a wonderful physical manifestation of that acting truth and, ultimately, every word out of your mouth is part of an "activity" because every word out of your mouth is part of something you are trying to achieve in that very moment. You can call this your action, your objective, your doing — *you can call it "Sam" if you want!* — as long as, eventually, you are in every moment actively pursuing, seeking and fighting for that which is essential to you! Of course, you must be struggling to accomplish something *while in continual adjustment to and in a moment-to-moment, authentic relationship with your partners on stage.*

But, there I go jumping ahead. Right now, we are only concerned with what you are getting from your partner in each moment and how what your partner does, affects you. *(The making choices in terms of what you are "doing" part of working with the text will come in my Meisner Workbook Four.)* So, in this way, the scene will actually be an improvisation in every way except that the words have been supplied to you by the playwright.

Some of you may experience some difficulty learning words, especially if you have not done much of it before. Here are some helpful ways to memorize words for you to try.

1. Use a blank index card or a folded piece of paper to cover the words of the script. Move the card or paper down to reveal one line of words. (I do not mean a whole sentence, I mean just one line of words in the script — or for you — in your re-

written script without punctuation.) Learn just that line. Then cover the line back up again and say those words without looking. Then move the card down again to check. Did you get it right? Exactly? If so, you may move the card down to reveal the next line of words. Learn that new line. Now cover both lines with the card and say the words – from the beginning – without looking. Then check the results. Did you get EVERY WORD correct? If so, move on to learn the next line. If you missed ANY WORD, you must start over from the beginning. That's right, from the very first word of the scene.

You will continue in this fashion until you have learned the entire scene. Remember, every time you learn a line, you go back to the very beginning of the scene and say every word you have learned so far. And, any time you miss a single word (whether you forget it or replace it with another word) you must start all over again from the beginning of the scene. Also, each time the card reveals a line that belongs to another character, simply read it to yourself and move on to your next line. You don't need to learn the other persons lines.

You will see that, in this manner, you will be repeating your words over and over and over again. The repetitive nature of this way of learning the words is very useful. Also, to make this very clear, I want you to learn the exact words of the scene. It is vital that you speak the words that the playwright wrote rather than para-phrasing or rewording the text.

2. Once you think you know the entire scene, get yourself some paper and pen. Using an index card again, cover your entire first line in the play (up until someone else talks,) and write your words on the paper. Then uncover the line from the script and check to see if you were 100% correct. If you missed a single word, go back and do it again. Work your way through the scene in this manner until you have written all of your words from the scene without any mistakes. Again, if you miss a single word, you must begin from the top and write every word over again.

This is really very much like the first way of learning words except that I have added writing to the mix. I find that the writing down of the words really helps "plant" the words in us in a deeper way.

3. Here's one that I don't use myself but I know actors who find it useful. Simply write down all of your words from the scene as if they were one long run-on sentence. So you would not include any of the lines that the other characters speak. Then you learn the words as if it were one single speech. The actors who do this tell me that it helps them not anticipate when the other actor is going to say their lines. Try it. If it works for you, great. If not, throw it out.

What's next? Soon, I'll want you to learn the words of our scene by rote.

But first, let's do a little practice session. Here are two short speeches. The first for men and the second for women. I want you to learn one of the speeches by rote so that you can just spit the words out rapidly with no acting, no inflections, no nothing — just words. After you think you really know the words, read on in the book.

And, before you learn the speech, you're going to do what? That's right, re-write the speech without punctuation.

MEN
From Horton Foote's *The Oil Well*

Will: I know we have. I've been saying it for twenty-eight years, and I know it's so. We're going to be rich men before we die. I couldn't sleep last night for thinking about it. It's the justification of my faith as I see it. I've held on to my land in spite of debt and fire and flood. Sometimes I'd be so tired I couldn't stand the thought of looking at another row of cotton, but every day when I went out to plow or to plant I'd say, don't give up. Hold on. There's oil here and you're gonna be rich.

WOMEN
From Horton Foote's *The Roads To Home*

Annie: Yes ma'am. I started home. Mr Long put me on the streetcar for home, and he took the streetcar for downtown. I had just gotten past the first stop when I looked around and saw I didn't have my children, so I said to the conductor stop this streetcar at once. Madam, he said, I can't stop it until the next corner. At once, I said, I have lost my children. I am in distress. Oh, I am sorry, he said, and he stopped the streetcar and I got off and I went running back to the stop on the opposite side of the street to wait for the next car going to your house, but then I got frantic and I thought what will my two little children think of their mother going off and leaving them, so I ran back here every step of the way.

• • •

Got the words down cold? Here's what I want you to do.

1. Say the speech three times in a row out loud. Say it as quickly as you can possibly talk and without any pauses. So, no pauses within the speech and no pauses when you start the speech over again for the second and third times. The only time it is okay to pause is when you run out of air and need to take in some more air so that you can continue speaking. Even then, breathe in quickly and continue talking. If you have to stop to try and remember a word, you must start over and do the speech three more times.

2. Once you are able to do the above little test, do the speech three times in the same manner while you are doing any activity that demands your attention. (Playing tennis or ping pong, slicing potatoes, balancing a broom on the tip of your thumb, etc.) Again, if you pause to remem-

ber, you must start the speech over again and do it three more times.

· · ·

If you have completed those two little "do I really know the word" tests, you should have a better understanding of what I mean by learning the words by rote and really knowing the words. By the way, I suggest that you read those two beautiful plays by Horton Foote. Are you starting to get the idea that I absolutely adore and treasure Horton's plays? YES I DO!

Okay. Now, I want you to learn the words of the scene we are working on. Use all of the ways we have just talked about and experimented with to learn the words by rote and to get those words in you so that they come out of your mouth as effortlessly as breathing, as "thought-less" as tying your shoes.

After you learn the words, I want you to move forward in the book and read assignment number eight which will give you instructions for working reading number four.

adding repetition

I want you and your partner to get back together now and do your next working reading. This will be the last working reading in which you have the script in front of you. (So this will be a good test to see if you really know those words!) In the fourth working reading, you will do the following:

1. Both partners leave their scripts on the table and go out of the room to prepare.

2. When you are fully prepared, come into the room and sit down. If you are the first one to come into the room, sit at the table and continue your preparation until your partner enters.

3. Once you are both at the table, leave the preparation alone and begin the working reading. Again, when I say to "leave the preparation alone," I am saying that you must stop the fanta-

sizing or free associating about your imaginary circumstances and you must now give your complete attention to your partner. In this way, you can allow yourself to "ride" fully on what the preparation has induced in you and to work off of what you are getting from your partner in each moment.

In addition to that, I will add one new element to the working reading:

4. When you have the impulse to, with the words from the script, use repetition to take you to the next moment. *(A note from Larry: "Repetition" is taught in my first book on the Meisner work, The Sanford Meisner Approach: An Actor's Workbook.)*

As a means of explaining myself, let's shift back into the classroom where Darby and Marvin have prepared, come into the room, are sitting at the table and now begin their working reading with repetition:

Marvin: what in gods name do you think you're doing

Darby: i'm packing

Marvin: you're packing

Darby: i'm packing don't you have any eyes in your head i'm packing

Marvin: well you can stop packing stop it right now

Darby: stop it right now

Marvin: stop it right now

Darby: out of my way

Marvin: you're being ridiculous

Darby: i'm being ridiculous

Marvin: you're being ridiculous it's late and hotels are expensive

Darby: i'm not going to a hotel i'm going home

Marvin: you're going home

Darby: i'm going home

Marvin: good grief home to mother minerva pinney returns to mama and the ancestral homestead you disappoint me darling this started out as a good honest row but now you're being commonplace

Darby: i'm being commonplace

Marvin: you're being commonplace

Darby: i'm not you're darling and i never want to see you again and please go in the other room

Marvin: and don't cry in the name of heaven don't cry tears will get you nowhere you merely look messy

Darby: i look messy

Marvin: you look messy

*Darby: adam why didn't you pay the light bill i gave you
the money*

*Marvin: how many times do i have to tell you i forgot i
completely forgot*

Darby: you completely forgot

Marvin: i completely forgot

Darby: but you spent the money

*Marvin: of course i spent the money if i find ten dollars in
my pocket and i need books i buy books what's wrong
with that*

Darby: what's wrong with that

*Marvin: yea whats wrong with that besides i can take
them out of my income tax*

Darby: your income tax

Marvin: my income tax

*Darby: what income you can't even get an advance from
your publisher any more they printed three thousand
copies of your last book and two thousand are being
remaindered in the drug stores*

Marvin: don't be a snob i write for the people

Darby: you write for the people

Marvin: i write for the people and where do you find the people in the drug stores

Darby: adam harwick the great historian a lipstick a tube of toothpaste and a forty nine cent biography of aaron burr will there be anything else madame

Darby and Marvin continue in this manner. And now, through the magic of my Motorola Mac computer, we leap ahead in time as Darby and Marvin are just completing their working reading with repetition...

Larry: That was very well done, very nice. I see that your preparations for beginning the scene are taking root and your use of the repetition to explore the scene was also handled well. *(Larry turns to the class.)* Tell me how Darby and Marvin incorporated the repetition into the working reading.

Ann: Well, I saw that they didn't repeat every word from the scene. They seemed to repeat any time they felt like it even if it was in the middle of the other person's line.

Larry: That's right, they didn't over do it or force it. They repeated whenever a moment had some meaning to them. In other words, they repeated whenever they had the impulse to. In this way, they were able to freely explore the meaning of the scene in new ways with each other. And, as you said, they didn't wait for the other person to finish a line, they jumped in and repeated whenever they wanted.

This reminds me of something that Sandy used to talk about. He told us that a "cue" isn't a technical thing. For those of you who don't know the term, a cue is the moment where you are supposed to start speaking your line or do something. Although many directors and actors think that "picking up your cue" is a technical thing, it isn't. Your "cue" always comes, as in life, from the need to respond. And that's not technical! You will see many actors who only "act" when they are saying their lines. When the other person is speaking, they stand there like a log doing nothing more than waiting for their next turn to say some more of their wonderful lines. Of course, this is not acting. *(Eddie waves his hand.)* Yes, Eddie.

Eddie: I also loved that the scene was like a roller coaster and that the repetition really kept Darby and Marvin in very close contact. Not just that, it brought up in them all kinds of responses to each other that I have never seen before when they have done their previous working readings... what I am trying to say is, that the scene took on a great sense of reality. There were times that I forgot I was watching a scene.

Larry: That's great. You know, ultimately, what we hope for is that the audience members do forget that they are watching a play and that they will feel like they are looking through a little peephole because what is happening between the actors *right now* and which the audience is witnessing *right now,* is so absolutely private. But, excuse me Eddie... *(Larry returns to you, the reader.)*

Okay, I think the use of the repetition should be clear enough to you now. Listen, don't make a big deal about this next step. Use the repetition freely and have some fun with it. AND WORK OFF EACH OTHER, RIGHT? So, get to work and when you have done the working reading with repetition, continue onto the next assignment.

putting the scene on its feet

Now it's time to move on to working reading number five, the last of the working readings, which will act as a bridge taking you from doing the scene in your seats to getting the scene fully on its feet. Before you do this working reading, I want to give you a way to warm up with your partner. It's called a *line rehearsal*.

It's very simple, here's how it goes:

Get a small pillow or a tennis ball or a stuffed animal or any other object you can throw without hurting someone. Stand about ten feet apart and start throwing the object back and forth rapidly. While you are tossing the object, begin spitting out the words of the scene as fast as you can say them – AND – with *no acting, no meaning*. Remember, say the words as fast as you can with no pauses between when your partner ends their line and when you begin yours. NO PAUSES! Do this until the two of you have completed the entire scene.

This is a very playful way to do a refresher on the words and to get in contact with your partner right before you are going to work on the scene together. It's energizing and fun — enjoy each other! I suggest you do a line rehearsal in this manner every time you get together to work. It's a great way to begin shifting from everything that has happened in your life during the day and into the world of the play you are about to inhabit together.

In this last working reading you will do the following:

1. Both partners go out of the room to prepare. Now that you really know the words, you are no longer using your scripts.

2. When you are fully prepared, come into the room and sit down. If you are the first one to come into the room, sit at the table and continue your preparation until your partner enters.

3. Once you are both at the table, leave the preparation alone and begin the working reading.

Here's the new instruction:

4. When either of you have the inpulse to, the "need" to, you may get up from the table and move. I am saying that, as you work off of each other, you must now allow yourself to do whatever you are moved to do. You are not tied to those chairs anymore! And of course, it's not about moving because you think you should move, it's about moving because you must!

Go ahead and do this working reading number five and then continue on to the next assignment.

a full improvisation

Well, this one's up to you, folks. Now it's time for you to do the scene:

- with your activity,
- with your preparations,
- and coming into the room.

So, the actress playing Minerva gets her room set up. Then, you both go out and prepare.

Make sure to leave the door open so that Minerva can close it when she comes in to pack her belongings. In this way, as we did previously in the exercises, the actor playing Adam will know when he can come in and begin the scene.

Remember, there is no "right way" for the scene to go. There is only "working off" each other and allowing yourself to respond fully to what the other person gives you.

There it is.

Get to work!

more delicious scenes for your acting pleasure

scene one

In this section of the book, I am going to give you some tasty and demanding scenes to sink your teeth into. The first two scenes come from a play that I love and which I had a blast directing two years ago at my theatre in Seattle. The play is *Shivaree* by William Mastrosimone. First I will give you the text of the scenes just as it appears in the play and then, for the first scene, I will give you some things to think about as you begin working on it. For the second scene, I won't interject my own thoughts, I'll let you tackle it on your own.

The first scene comes from the beginning of the play and is a two man scene. The second scene is for a man and a woman. If you choose to work with a partner on only one of the scenes, I suggest that you work on the assignments I will give you for both of the scenes. If you decide not to actually work with a partner on either of the scenes, I still want you to do the writing assignments that will be given here in the book so that you keep strengthening your skills in investigating the script. Oh yes, and whether you are a woman or a man, do the assignments for all three of the characters we get to meet in these two scenes.

As we did earlier, we will work on these scenes out of context of the play. What I mean is, we will work only with the information we are given in the scenes themselves. (As we get into the more advanced elements of interpretation, in my *Meisner Approach Workbook Four*, we will investigate and grapple with the entire play.) After you finish this book, I urge you to read *Shivaree* and the other wonderful plays by William Mastrosimone. My publishers, Smith and Kraus, have put together a terrific collection of his plays.

Oh yes, after you have worked on these two scenes, I have a very yummy bonus scene for you!

Ready? It's time to read the first scene.

. . .

SCENE ONE
Shivaree by William Mastrosimone
The Characters: Chandler and Scagg

(Chandler turns the music off, opens a bag, takes out an ascot, peels off sales tag, puts it on, puts on Johnny Mathis, stands before his mirror.)

Chandler: How do you do? Won't you sit down? *(New pose.)* How do you do? Won't you sit down? *(Turns off the music, opens artbook of Botticelli's paintings; to himself — simply because the sound pleases him:)*

Simonetta. *(He gets a "Playboy" out of hiding, compares, and recites as if cramming for an exam.)* Mons veneris. Labia majora. Labia minora. Mucus membrane secretes a viscous fluid when stimulated which acts as a lubricant and thus facilitates copulation. One hundred and forty million. One hundred and forty million. A million is a thousand thousands. And that times 140 is one hundred and forty million sperms per ejaculation. I am one out of one hundred and forty million. It's like the Boston Marathon! And I won! *(The buzzer rings. He rushes to it.)* Who's there?

Scagg: *(Over intercom:)* Fudgie wudgie, creamsicle, Eskimo pie, fur pie!

Chandler: Are you alone?

Scagg: Open up, amigo.

(Chandler releases the door lock, puts on his suit jacket, preens up. Enter Scagg in white pants, white shirt, white shoes and panama hat with a feather lugging a metal box on shoulder straps with cartoon characters painted on the side.)

Scagg: M'man! m'man! M'main man!

Chandler: Where is she?

Scagg: The whore is in the truck and I'm double parked. — Lay alittle cash on me, bro.

Chandler: Let me open the wine so it can breathe.
(Scagg opens the metal box, takes out a brown liquor store bag.)

Scagg: Let there be juice!

Chandler: What is this?

Scagg: The wine.

Chandler: This isn't Medoc.

Scagg: Medoc? I thought you said Mad Dog.

Chandler: I never heard of this! Where's the corkscrew!

Scagg: This is 20th century technology — you don't need one for this wine, Amigo.

Chandler: O God, Scagg! This is awful!

Scagg: What's the button here? Quick k.o.? For a five-spot more you got genuine mountain corn brew. Goes down hot, lays 'em out cold. *(Taking a mason jar of clear moonshine from the metal box.)* — On special.

Chandler: I don't want that!

Scagg: Fudgie-wudgie?

Chandler: No! Did you forget the candles?

Scagg: Only the best for my m'man! *(Taking votive candles from the box.)*

Chandler: These are used! Where'd you get these?

Scagg: The church on the corner.

Chandler: You robbed these from the church!

Scagg: Hell, m'man, they had a whole shitload.

Chandler: O, God, Scagg.

Scagg: M'man, these are consecrated.

Chandler: Did you tell her about, you know, me?

Scagg: Yup.

Chandler: How'd you tell her?

Scagg: Just like you told me.

Chandler: How?

Scagg: I said I got a friend, he's a hypodermiac . . .

Chandler: Hemophiliac.

Scagg: Right. Right.

Chandler: And what was her reaction?

Scagg: Gooseegg.

Chandler: Really? What color's her hair?

Scagg: Just like you wanted.

Chandler: She pretty?

Scagg: Pretty?

Chandler: Really?

Scagg: Any man with red blood in his vein would crawl five
     hundred miles on hands and knees over broken bottles
     and armadilla turds just to'hear this enchalada burp.

Chandler: O, God, Scagg, she's not cheap, is she?

Scagg: Fifty bucks.

Chandler: No! Is she slutty-looking?

Scagg: In her spare time she poses for madonna pictures.

Chandler: How long's her hair?

Scagg: About here.

Chandler: That's-short!

Scagg: Whattaya gonna do with a hank o'hair?

Chandler: I asked you to regard that!

Scagg: You want hair, I'll get you a sheepdog cheaper.

Chandler: I specifically stipulated length and color.

Scagg: M'man, it ain't like shopping at the A&P.

Chandler: Does she look like this? *(Showing the Botticelli book.)*

Scagg: That what you want? A born-again Billy Gramm girl?

Chandler: She's not like this? What's so funny?

Scagg: One leg's longer than the other.

Chandler: She's not like this?

Scagg: Alittle. Only thing, she's got a very mild case of herpes.

Chandler: O God!

Scagg: C'mon, bro! I'm only goosin ya!

Chandler: Everything's gone awry!

(Scagg rolls back his long sleeve, revealing a dozen watches.)

Scagg: I got a good deal on a watch.

Chandler: I don't want a watch! What will the cost be for, you know, just the woman?

Scagg: Fifty.

Chandler: I don't mean to impugn your integrity, but is that normal?

Scagg: Plus ten for the vino.

Chandler: For that?

Scagg: Candles on me. And five for this. *(Taking out a packet from the box.)* This'll drive her t'loonsville, jack. French tickler.

Chandler: I don't want that.

Scagg: Take the watch, I throw in the tickler.

Chandler: No.

Scagg: Want another magazine?

Chandler: No.

Scagg: Then we're up to fifty plus ten, – that's sixty five dollars.

Chandler: Sixty.

Scagg: Right, plus ten for my time. Seventy. Grass?

Chandler: No.

Scagg: Coke?

Chandler: No.

Scagg: Just askin. *(Chandler goes to a hiding place, takes out a pillow case filled with coins of every denomination neatly wrapped. Scagg takes out a tiny tin.)* Tiger balm?

Chandler: What's that?

Scagg: Tiger balm. Extract from the horn of the white rhino. Gives ya a stone bone.

Chandler: I don't want an aphrodisiac.

Scagg: 'Course ya don't. Not now. Don't need an umbrella when the sun's shinin, do ya?

Chandler: How much?

Scagg: Now, m'man, there's three, four, maybe five rhinoes rottin on the plains o'Sergengeti t'fill this little tin – but it's enough for half a lifetime.

Chandler: How much?

Scagg: Top shelf, m'man. Seventy-five.

Chandler: Can I owe it to you?

Scagg: Nothin' walks 'less the president talks.

Chandler: Can't afford it.

Scagg: My cost – twenty five.

Chandler: Can't afford it.

Mary: *(On c.b.)* Mobile to Home Base, c'mon.

Chandler: Stand still! Don't breathe! She's got ears! Home Base to Mobile, over.

Mary: Wattcha doin, babe? Over.

Chandler: Reading. Over.

Mary: Want some ice cream? Over.

Chandler: Negatory, Mom, but thanks. What's your 10-20?

Mary: Just dropped off a fare downtown, honey babe. Conventioneers are comin' on like locusts. Catch ya on the flip-flop, honey babe.

Chandler: Forty Rodger.

Scagg: Gimmie the money — I'll bring her up.

Chandler: Could we postpone this?

Scagg: Goddamn, I went out of my way to get you a woman — not just a woman, but one with hair, and this, and that. Damn, boy, you know how much business I lost?

Chandler: I'm sorry.

Scagg: Sorry ain't gonna help me pay your mama the rent tomorrow.

Chandler: She suspects something.

Scagg: Use my room.

Chandler: But if I'm not here when she calls, she'll come looking.

Scagg: She won't look for you there. You leave by the roomer's entrance, come back in your private entrance. Say you went for a walk.

Chandler: Oh...I don't know...

Scagg: Now you decide right now if you wanna ride or slide.

Chandler: I planned this for a year!

Scagg: Ride or slide.

Chandler: Ride.

Scagg: Lay some cash on me bro. — What's that?

Chandler: The money.

Scagg: Don't you have paper?

Chandler: I've hoarded loose change for over a year. It's the only way I get money. For the ice cream.

Scagg: How am I gonna pay her with 97 pounds o'coin?

Chandler: Ten, twenty, thirty, forty.

Scagg: This is a real ass-pain.

Chandler: Fifty, sixty, sixty-five, seventy.

Scagg: This is a real snafu, m'man.

Chandler: Should we postpone it?

Scagg: I don't know if she's gonna take it.

Chandler: Wait!

Scagg: What?

Chandler: I have to ask you something.

Scagg: You want the tickler.

Chandler: No! When you bring her up...

Scagg: Yeah.

Chandler: And you leave us, right?

Scagg: Not 'less you want me t'cheerlead...Chandler, Chandler, he's m'man, if he can't do it...

Chandler: Scagg! C'mon! This is important!

Scagg: Sorry, Amigo.

Chandler: When it's just me and her, what do I do? – I mean, I know what to do, but – how would you, say, get things started?

Scagg: Hang loose, drink a little juice, and the one-eyed worm'll find it's way home.

Chandler: Scagg, concerning the actual womanly part?

Scagg: Yeah.

Chandler: Could we possibly discuss that a little?

Scagg: I can talk all night about the vertical smile. I seen dogs rip open jugglers for it; bulls break down barn doors for it; roosters chew chicken wire t'get in the coop. I seen cowboys get throwed off a brama – o'purpose! – just t'snag the fancy o'some freckled little pony tail up in the bleechers! You can't name the things a

male won't do for that little patch o'real estate no big-
ger than a fried egg.

Chandler: What was that?

Scagg: What?

Chandler: My mother's cab. She just pulled up.

Scagg: Holy shit!

Chandler: Go down the back way. We'll do it another
night.

Scagg: No, I'll bring the woman when your mama goes.

. . .

Before you get to work, let's clear something up. I told
you this was a two person scene. But, as you read it, you discovered that Mary comes along on the c.b. Don't make a big
deal out of this. Simply have some kind of microphone for
Chandler to use and have one of your classmates or acting
partners read the part of Mary from her seat in class.

Now, if you are going to actually work on this or any of
the scenes, what will you do with the scene before you do
anything else? Good answer! (See how confident I am in
you!) That's right, you will re-write the scene without
punctuation and stage directions. Next, I want you to complete the following written assignments.

1. COMPARE THE SCENE TO THE EXERCISE

a) Who is in the room?

_____

_____

b) What is his activity?

_____

_____

c) Who is coming to the door?

_____

_____

d) What is bringing him to the door?

_____

_____

_____

_____

_____

e) What is their relationship?

_____

_____

_____

Here are my answers:

a) Chandler is in his room.

b) His activity is getting ready for his first sexual experience.

c) Scagg is coming to the door.

d) What we know is that Scagg has achieved getting Chandler everything he has asked for. More importantly, we know that Scagg now wants to get paid. The scene doesn't tell us why he needs the money, but for some specific and meaningful reason, he's got to collect on the "job" now! (We will talk more about this later.)

e) Chandler is the son of the landlord and Scagg is a tenant who lives in their house and who provides Chandler with things like skin-magazines, etc.

2. WHAT IS THE EMOTIONAL PREPARATION

Talk about the nature of the emotional preparation each actor would have to do to begin the scene and how you arrived at your answer.

Chandler:

_____

_____

_____

_____

_____

_____

_____

_____

_____

_____

_____

_____

_____

_____

_____

_____

_____

_____

_____

_____

Scagg:

_____

_____

_____

_____

_____

_____

_____

_____

_____

_____

_____

_____

_____

_____

_____

_____

_____

_____

_____

_____

_____

_____

_____

_____

_____

_____

Here are my notes:

Chandler: The actor playing Chandler must be exhilarated and excited to begin the scene. I came to this answer because in the scene I find out that this night is the culmination of a year of getting ready for it. Chandler says:

"I planned this for a year"

Also, when Scagg asks for paper money, Chandler tells him:

"I've hoarded loose change for over a year. It's the only way I get money. For the ice cream."

When you consider this grown man, (just in case you wondered, Chandler is an adult) who has clearly never been with a woman, saving up his nickels and dimes for a year so that he could create this transformational evening, you can imagine the kind of adrenaline-pumping condition he must be in. And, it's happening! Tonight! Everything he has fantasized about, studied in his books — and tonight his dreams are fulfilled. Wouldn't you say he's in a buoyant and excited state? As he says:

"I am one out of one hundred and forty million. It's like the Boston Marathon! And I won!"

Scagg: The actor playing Scagg begins the scene in a victorious state. One way of looking at it is that he has been sent on a vital mission and he has come back having achieved everything he was sent out to do. From Scagg's point of view, and with the reasons he has for accepting the mission, don't you think that's true? Well, now he comes to collect his reward! And for Scagg, the reward is what it is all about. Victory is sweet!

Also, when you think about making money, what's going to get Scagg the biggest payoff — being apologetic because he couldn't find a bottle of Medoc and the prostitute he found doesn't have the right kind of hair? OR, coming in TOTALLY CONFIDENT AND ENTHUSIASTIC because he has COMPLETELY FULFILLED CHANDLER'S EVERY DESIRE!

3. WHAT IS OF IMPORTANCE TO EACH CHARACTER:

Explore what is of meaning to Chandler and Scagg. Remember, don't conjecture or assume — the script is your Bible!

CHANDLER

_____

_____

_____

_____

_____

_____

_____

_____

_____

_____

_____

_____

_____

_____

_____

_____

_____

_____

_____

_____

_____

_____

_____

CHANDLER

_____

_____

_____

_____

_____

_____

_____

_____

_____

_____

_____

_____

_____

_____

_____

_____

_____

_____

_____

_____

_____

_____

_____

_____

SCAGG

_____

_____

_____

_____

_____

_____

_____

_____

_____

_____

_____

_____

_____

_____

_____

_____

_____

_____

_____

_____

_____

_____

_____

_____

_____

_____

SCAGG

_____

_____

_____

_____

_____

_____

_____

_____

_____

_____

_____

_____

_____

_____

_____

_____

_____

_____

_____

_____

_____

_____

_____

_____

Here are my notes:

CHANDLER

To me, there are really three key issues for Chandler. First, that he is fully prepared for what is about to happen here this evening. (It's taken a year to make this night happen and he cannot afford to make any mistakes!) Second, that the evening meets up to his romantic vision and expectations. And third, that the woman understands and is accepting of his condition. Let's look at these things together.

A. Being Prepared

Obviously, Chandler is very concerned about being fully prepared for his first evening alone with a woman. The first thing we see Chandler doing is practicing the best ways to greet his "date" when she arrives:

> *Chandler: How do you do? Won't you sit down? (New pose.) How do you do? Won't you sit down?*

Chandler also wants to be prepared for the sexual part of the evening, so he makes sure that he remembers the technical aspects of being with a woman:

> *Chandler: Mons veneris. Labia majora. Labia minora. Mucus membrane secretes a viscous fluid when stimulated which acts as a lubricant and thus facilitates copulation.*

Also, concerning the sex part, Chandler asks Scagg for advice about what to do once the woman is actually here:

Chandler: I have to ask you something.

Scagg: You want the tickler.

Chandler: No! When you bring her up . . .

Scagg: Yeah.

Chandler: And you leave us, right?

Scagg: Not 'less you want me t'cheerlead . . .Chandler, Chandler, he's m'man, if he can't do it . . .

Chandler: Scagg! C'mon! This is important!

Scagg: Sorry, Amigo.

Chandler: When it's just me and her, what do I do? — I mean, I know what to do, but — how would you, say, get things started?

Scagg: Hang loose, drink a little juice, and the one-eyed worm'll find its way home.

Chandler: Scagg, concerning the actual womanly part?

Scagg: Yeah.

Chandler: Could we possibly discuss that a little?

B. Creating a truly romantic evening

Chandler has a very specific romantic image of how he wants the evening to look, sound and feel. It is in pursuit of fulfilling this fantasy that he has enlisted Scagg's help. And, every element is vital to Chandler. Let's look at these elements.

THE WINE:

Chandler: Let me open the wine so it can breathe.

Scagg: Let there be juice!

Chandler: This isn't Medoc.

Scagg: Medoc? I thought you said Mad Dog.

Chandler: I never heard of this! Where's the corkscrew!

Scagg: This is 20th century technology — you don't need one for this wine, Amigo.

Chandler: O God, Scagg! This is awful!

THE CANDLES:

Chandler: Did you forget the candles?

Scagg: Only the best for mm'man!

Chandler: These are used! Where'd you get these?

Scagg: You robbed these from the church!

Scagg: Hell, m'man, they had a whole shitload.

Chandler: O, God, Scagg.

THE "BOTTICELLI TYPE" WOMAN:

Chandler: What color's her hair?

Scagg: Just like you wanted.

Chandler: She pretty?

Scagg: Pretty?

Chandler: Really?

Scagg: Any man with red blood in his vein would crawl five hundred miles on hands and knees over broken beer bottles and armadilla turds just to'hear this enchilada burp.

Chandler: O, God, Scagg, she's not cheap, is she?

Scagg: Fifty bucks.

Chandler: No! Is she slutty looking?

Scagg: In her spare time she poses for madonna pictures.

Chandler: How long's her hair?

Scagg: About here.

Chandler: That's — short!

Scagg: Whattaya gonna do with a hank o'hair?

Chandler: I asked you to regard that!

Scagg: You want hair, I'll get ya a sheepdog cheaper.

Chandler: I specifically stipulated length and color.

Scagg: M'man, it ain't like shopping at the A&P.

Chandler: Does she look like this? (Showing the Botticelli book.)

Scagg: That what you want? A born-again Billy Gramm girl?

Chandler: She's not like this? What's so funny?

Scagg: One leg's longer than the other.

Chandler: She's not like this?

C. That the Woman Understands and Accepts His Condition

It may be a brief statement in the scene, but I say it is very important to Chandler that the woman knows about and is ok with the fact that Chandler is a hemophiliac.

Chandler: Did you tell her about, you know, me?

Scagg: Yup.

Chandler: How'd you tell her?

Scagg: Just like you told me.

Chandler: How?

Scagg: I said I got a friend, he's a hypodermiac . . .

Chandler: Hemophiliac.

Scagg: Right. Right.

Chandler: And what was her reaction?

Scagg: Gooseegg.

Chandler: Really?

SCAGG

If we look at everything Scagg does in this scene, it becomes pretty obvious that he is interested in one main thing — getting as much money out of Chandler as possible! Look, what is the first thing that Scagg does when he enters? He tries to get the money!

Scagg: M'man! m'man! M'main man!

Chandler: Where is she?

Scagg: The whore's in the truck and I'm double parked. Lay a little cash on me, bro.

Obviously, Scagg wants Chandler to give him the money quickly. I doubt if Scagg would have stuck around or turned over any of the items he gives to Chandler if Chandler had paid him right away. To me, the scene we have between Scagg and Chandler in the play was really Scagg's "Plan B" which Scagg implements when Chandler doesn't "lay a little cash" on him immediately. I mean, do you think Scagg is concerned for Chandler or truly interested in his needs? It's pretty clear that he isn't, right?

Now, as I said when we talked about how this scene compares to an exercise, we don't know the specific reasons that Scagg needs the money. But it is up to you, the actor, to make that reason important and important RIGHT NOW! I don't think we need to review all the things that Scagg tries to sell Chandler during the course of the scene and I don't want to complicate something that is very straightforward.

4. WORK WITH YOUR PARTNER!

Before you get to work, I want you to write a list of every "thing" you will need to actually do this scene. (And this scene happens to have a lot of "things!") For example, you will need a book of Botticelli paintings, a bottle of cheap wine, tiger balm, etc... So take a piece of paper and write down every prop you will need before you can fully get this scene on its feet. Of course, even though I won't mention it again, you must do this for all of the scenes you work on.

Now you may continue with your series of:

· mechanical readings,
· working readings,
· learning the words by rote,
· adding repetition,
· putting the scene on its feet,
· and then having a full improvisation with the scene.

Enjoy!

scene two

Shivaree by William Mastrosimone
The Characters: Chandler and Laura

Laura: Hi.

Chandler: Won't you sit down?

Laura: I am.

Chandler: At the table?

Laura: Oh, you like it on the table?

Chandler: No. No. I mean . . .

Laura: Look, I understand. I do a guy who's into closets.

Chandler: No, I mean for a drink of wine or tea or...that's
all I have. Scagg brought this wine. Not having drunk it,
I can't testify as to its merits.

Laura: What's the matter?

Chandler: I don't remember where I hid it. I didn't want my ...well, actually I wanted to put it where it wouldn't get broken.

Laura: Scagg said it's goodnight if you get cut.

Chandler: That's not true.

Laura: I had a client do a massive coronary on me once. Thing was, I didn't know and kept going.

Chandler: I wish I could remember...I was here and...

Laura: That's ok. I don't need any wine.

Chandler: Do you like music?

Laura: I'd gut my dog if I thought it'd make a good sound.

Chandler: What would you like to hear?

Laura: Whatever brings ya to a head, sweetheart. *(Chandler puts on a tape.)* You read all these books?

Chandler: Yes.

Laura: I like brains.

Chandler: Pardon?

Laura: Brains. I like em.

Chandler: I'm a bibliophile.

Laura: O, I'm sorry.

(The music comes on. Laura bursts out laughing.)

Chandler: Would you prefer something else?

Laura: No, love, it's fabulous. Relax.

Chandler: I am.

Laura: No you're not. Really. Let yourself go.

Chandler: Thank you.

Laura: Let's sit on the bed and talk about it.

Chandler: Momentarily.

Laura: It's alright, love, 'least you don't want t'pour teryaki sauce all over me.

Chandler: Pardon?

Laura: Nothin'. You still looking for that wine?

Chandler: Yes.

Laura: Wouldn't you rather undress me?

Chandler: I would really like to have some wine first.

Laura: You wanna do this some other time?

Chandler: Would that be inconvenient?

Laura: I'm booked all week what with the A.M.A. and Shriners conventions.

Chandler: No. Now. Tonight.

Laura: So we gotta rise to the occasion 'cause I got other people to see.

Chandler: O.

Laura: You thought I'd stay all night?

Chandler: Well, yes.

Laura: It's a hundred big ones for all night, babe.

Chandler: I didn't know.

Laura: Otherwise, it's thirty-five a throw.

Chandler: Thirty-five?

Laura: For a straight jump.

Chandler: What else's, you know, available?

Laura: Well, there's straight, half and half, doggie-doggie, 'round the world.

Chandler: Fine.

Laura: You want the works?

Chandler: Sure.

Laura: Whoa, wild man, — that's two hundred and fifty plus mucho stamina.

Chandler: O. O, I see. Let's...just regular.

Laura: Well, let's get the fish in the pan here, babe.

Chandler: I'm not quite ready.

Laura: Want me to talk filthy?

Chandler: No. Thank you.

Laura: Wis un accent, eh, amor?

Chandler: Thank you just the same.

Laura: Wanna just shoot the breeze awhile?

Chandler: Would that be possible?

Laura: Walter used to have to talk first.

Chandler: Walter?

Laura: Philosophy Proff, Tuesday nights.

Chandler: Really? What's he talk about?

Laura: Talked about them Greek boys and diabolical materialism. Hooked up a garden hose to the exhaust pipe, sat in the back seat, and there went my education. – So what should we talk about?

Chandler: Why did he kill himself?

Laura: The man had a thing about, you know, reality...all that about – I can think therefore I'm here.

Chandler: "I think therefore I am."

Laura: They changed it?

Chandler: No. It's still the same.

Laura: So, let's talk about the planets. – What's that?

Chandler: That's an artist's conception of the origin of our universe. It's called the BIG BANG THEORY.

Laura: I know that theory. Feel better? Good. Let's go.

Chandler: Please! — Please don't squeeze my wrist so hard.

Laura: What'd I do?

Chandler: I bruise quite easily.

Laura: Jesus. What is this thing you've got?

Chandler: Blood disorder. Not contagious. Inherited. Actually it's the lack of a protein in the blood plasma which regulates the time it takes for blood to clot.

Laura: That's a real bitch. Can I undress you?

Chandler: *(Pause.)* Yes

(She begins to undress him.)

Laura: What a fine ascot. Silk? Relax. Your neck's so tight. Let your arms just hang down. Sure. Yes. Yes. Relax. Touch me. Not there. Somewheres else. Close your eyes. Close 'em. Shhh! Don't talk. Touch my belly. Yes. That's where it all is. You are such a lovely man.

(Mary's voice interrupts over c.b.)

Mary: *(On c.b.)* Mobile to Home Base, copy?

Laura: Police!

Chandler: Don't move! Please! Don't make a sound!

Laura: I'm on probation. You got a back door here? *(Grabbing her belongings in a rush.)*

Chandler: Please! It's my mom!

Mary: Mobile to Home Base, c'mon!

Chandler: Home base to Mobile, copy?

Mary: Wall to wall, treetop tall. Sorry to wake you sugar, but I'm taking some oil people over to the Palm Room and I won't be home till very late, so don't you worry none, k?

Chandler: OK.

Mary: Sugar? You brush your teeth?

Chandler: Yes, ma'm.

Mary: Dental floss?

Chandler: Yes, ma'm.

Mary: Brush 'em again, honeybabe.

Chandler: Yes, ma'm.

Mary: Night, night, lovy. Over.

Chandler: Good night. Over.

Laura: Your mama loves ya.

Chandler: I really need some wine.

Laura: You don't need wine. You need to come over here.

Chandler: I know it's right here! Somewhere!

Laura: And after wine you'll wanna brush your teeth and floss! Bonzo's gonna think I'm moonlighting.

Chandler: What are you doing?

Laura: Seducing you.

Chandler: O.

Laura: C'mon, lay your sweet head down on your nice white pillow.

Chandler: Pillow! *(He springs up from the pillow, finds the wine under it.)* Eureka! Would you like some?

Laura: Just a swig.

Chandler: Caps so tight.

Laura: You have to break the metal band first.

Chandler: I can't seem to . . .

Laura: Here.

Chandler: Oh, God.

Laura: You cut?

Chandler: On the cap.

Laura: Oh, shit, you gonna die now?

Chandler: My life is not that exciting.

Laura: Please don't die on me, cupcake.

Chandler: I'm fine.

Laura: Let me call an ambulance.

Chandler: No. I'm fine.

Laura: You faintin'?

Chandler: No.

Laura: Sure?

Chandler: Yes.

Laura: You look pale.

Chandler: I'm Caucasian. Thank you.

Laura: You're so cold.

Chandler: I have to rest now.

Laura: You ain't checkin out, are ya?

Chandler: No. Please go!

Laura: I'll come back some other time.

Chandler: Yes.

(Chandler gets into bed. Laura covers him.)

Laura: And we can talk about the stars and all.

Chandler: Yes.

Laura: And maybe you'd like to take Walter's Tuesday night slot.

Chandler: Please go.

Laura: Sweetie babe? I need the money.

Chandler: But nothing happened.

Laura: You pay for the time, not the ride, babe.

Chandler: I gave it to Scagg.

Laura: Scagg? He don't take the squirt, boy. I need some
  paper t' account my time t' Bonzo.
Chandler: Scagg's got it.

Laura: *(Grabbing his face.)* If you lie, me and Bonzo's coming back. *(Exit Laura.)*

. . .

Ready to get to work?

1. COMPARE THE SCENE TO THE EXERCISE

a) Who is in the room?

_____

_____

b) What is his activity?

_____

_____

c) Who is coming to the door?

_____

_____

d) What is bringing her to the door?

_____

_____

e) What is their relationship?

_____

_____

2. WHAT IS THE EMOTIONAL PREPARATION:

Chandler:

_____

_____

_____

_____

_____

_____

_____

Laura:

_____

_____

_____

_____

_____

_____

I said I wouldn't interject on the second scene. Woops, I lied. You know, not every entrance in every scene requires a true emotional preparation. Sometimes, it's enough to work from how you have assigned personal meaning to where you are coming from and the importance of what it is you are coming to do. That's what you must "know" and then leave alone. If you have made that specific for yourself and it has meaning to you, it will come up on its own during the course of the scene.

That's the case with Laura in this scene with Chandler. The actress playing Laura doesn't really have an emotional preparation. What she knows, and what will come up as the scene unfolds, is the importance of getting paid and how this relates to Bonzo. Even though Laura doesn't say a lot about Bonzo in this scene, she still makes it clear that, because of him, the money is important. And, as the actress, it's not just important — it must be personally CRUCIAL!

3. WHAT IS OF IMPORTANCE TO EACH CHARACTER:

CHANDLER

_____

_____

_____

_____

_____

_____

_____

_____

_____

_____

_____

_____

_____

_____

CHANDLER

_____

_____

_____

_____

_____

_____

_____

_____

_____

_____

_____

_____

_____

_____

_____

_____

_____

_____

_____

_____

_____

_____

_____

_____

_____

_____

_____

LAURA

_____

_____

_____

_____

_____

_____

_____

_____

_____

_____

_____

_____

_____

_____

_____

_____

_____

_____

_____

_____

_____

_____

_____

_____

LAURA

_____

_____

_____

_____

_____

_____

_____

_____

_____

_____

_____

_____

_____

_____

_____

_____

_____

_____

_____

_____

_____

_____

_____

_____

4. WORK WITH YOUR PARTNER!

Now you may continue with your series of mechanical readings, working readings, learning the words by rote, adding repetition, putting the scene on its feet and then having a full improvisation with the scene.

bonus scene

I said I had a bonus scene for you. Here it is. It's another beautiful scene from a Horton Foote play for you to work on. If you are a young woman, you will have the time of your life bringing this scene to life. For everyone else, this is a little treasure for all of you to enjoy.

A *Young Lady of Property* by Horton Foote
The Characters: Wilma and Arabella

(Wilma sits in the swing rocking back and forth. Arabella comes running in.)

Wilma: Hey, Arabella. Come sit and swing.

Arabella: All right. Your letter came.

Wilma: Whoopee. Where is it?

Arabella: Here.

(She gives it to her. Wilma tears it open. She reads.)

Wilma: *(Reading.)* Dear Miss Thompson: Mr. Delafonte will be glad to see you any time next week about your contemplated screen test. We suggest you call the office when you arrive in the city and we will set an exact time. Yours truly, Adele Murray. Well...Did you get yours?

Arabella: Yes.

Wilma: What did it say?

Arabella: The same.

Wilma: Exactly the same?

Arabella: Yes.

Wilma: Well, let's pack our bags. Hollywood, here we come.

Arabella: Wilma...

Wilma: Yes?

Arabella: I have to tell you something...Well...I...

Wilma: What is it?

Arabella: Well...promise me you won't hate me, or stop being my friend. I never had a friend, Wilma, until you began being nice to me, and I couldn't stand it if you weren't my friend any longer...

Wilma: Oh, my cow. Stop talking like that. I'll never stop being your friend. What do you want to tell me?

Arabella: Well...I don't want to go to see Mr. Delafonte, Wilma...

Wilma: You Don't?

Arabella: No. I don't want to be a movie star. I don't want to leave Harrison or my mother or father...I just want to stay here the rest of my life and get married and settle down and have children.

Wilma: Arabella...

Arabella: I just pretended like I wanted to go to Hollywood because I knew you wanted me to, and I wanted you to like me...

Wilma: Oh, Arabella...

Arabella: Don't hate me, Wilma. You see, I'd be afraid...I'd die if I had to go to see Mr. Delafonte. Why, I even get faint when I have to recite before the class. I'm not like you. You're not scared of anything.

Wilma: Why do you say that?

Arabella: Because you're not. I know.

Wilma: Oh, yes, I am. I'm scared of lots of things.

Arabella: What?

Wilma: Getting lost in a city. Being bitten by dogs. Old lady Leighton taking my daddy away...*(A pause.)*

Arabella: Will you still be my friend?

Wilma: Sure. I'll always be your friend.

Arabella: I'm glad. Oh, I almost forgot. Your Aunt Gert said for you to come on home.

Wilma: I'll go in a little. I love to swing in my front yard. Aunt Gert has a swing in her front yard, but it's not the same. Mama and I used to come out here and swing together. Some nights when Daddy was out all night gambling, I used to wake up and hear her out here swinging away. Sometimes she'd let me come and sit beside her. We'd swing until three or four in the morning. *(A pause. She looks out into the yard.)* The pear tree looks sickly, doesn't it? The fig trees are doing nicely though. I was out in the back and the weeds are near knee high, but fig trees just seem to thrive in the weeds. The freeze must have killed off the banana trees. ...*(A pause. Wilma stops swinging — she walks around the yard.)* Maybe I won't leave either. Maybe I won't go to Hollywood after all.

Arabella: You won't?

Wilma: No. Maybe I shouldn't. That just comes to me now. You know sometimes my old house looks so lonesome it tears at my heart. I used to think it looks lonesome just whenever it had no tenants, but now it comes to me it has looked lonesome ever since Mama died and we moved away, and it will look lonesome until some of us move back here. Of course, Mama can't, and Daddy won't. So it's up to me.

Arabella: Are you gonna live here all by yourself?

Wilma: No. I talk big about living here by myself, but I'm too much of a coward to do that. But maybe I'll finish school and live with Aunt Gert and keep on renting the house until I meet some nice boy with good habits and steady ways, and marry him. Then we'll move here and have children and I bet this old house won't be lonely any more. I'll get Mama's old croquet set and put it out under the pecan trees and play croquet with my children, or sit in this yard and swing and wave to people as they pass by.

Arabella: Oh, I wish you would. Mama says that's a normal life for a girl, marrying and having children. She says being an actress is all right, but the other's better.

Wilma: Maybe I've come to agree with your mama. Maybe I was going to Hollywood out of pure lonesomeness. I felt so alone with Mrs. Leighton getting my daddy and my mama having left the world. Daddy could have taken away my lonesomeness, but he didn't want to or couldn't. Aunt Gert says nobody is lonesome with a house full of children, so maybe that's what I just ought to stay here and have...

Arabella: Have you decided on a husband yet?

Wilma: No.

Arabella: Mama says that's the bad feature of being a girl, you have to wait for the boy to ask you and just pray that the one you want wants you. Tommy Murray is nice, isn't he?

Wilma: I think so.

Arabella: Jay Godfrey told me once he wanted to ask you for a date, but he didn't dare because he was afraid you'd turn him down.

Wilma: Why did he think that?

Arabella: He said the way you talked he didn't think you would go out with anything less than a movie star.

Wilma: Maybe you'd tell him different...

Arabella: All right. I think Jay Godfrey is very nice. Don't you?

Wilma: Yes, I think he's very nice and Tommy is nice...

Arabella: Maybe we could double-date sometimes.

Wilma: That might be fun.

Arabella: Oh, Wilma. Don't go to Hollywood. Stay here in Harrison and let's be friends forever...

Wilma: All right. I will.

Arabella: You will?

Wilma: Sure, why not? I'll stay here. I'll stay and marry and live in my house.

Arabella: Oh, Wilma. I'm so glad. I'm so very glad.

. . .

Now, as you compare this scene to the exercise and consider the emotional preparations, this scene presents a few fun things to grapple with. First of all, and obviously, there is no room, right? Well, it's the same thing. In this case, the "room" is actually outside the house and on the swing. Also, although Wilma doesn't seem to have the kind of "activity" we have worked on, she is alone at the beginning of the scene and she must be involved in "doing" something. Remember, "ACTING IS DOING" and when you are not doing something specific, you are no longer acting.

So, what might Wilma be involved in, what might she be "doing" as she is sitting on the swing alone? I'll give you a hint. By "doing," I don't mean reading a book or sewing. I don't even mean anything outwardly physical. I'll give you another hint. Do you remember one of the first exercises I did with you way back at the beginning of our sessions together in Workbook One? It was an illustration of the reality of doing. For those of you who haven't done it, I'll give it to you again right now. Do this:

In your mind, not on paper, in your mind's eye, I want you to multiply the following two numbers — 6497 X 3328. Go ahead and close your eyes and multiply those two numbers in your mind.

6497 X 3328

Do it now, then read on.

• • •

Now, if you really tried to do that, to multiply those two numbers — even though you may not have arrived at an answer — you just experienced what it is to be involved in really doing something. And, if I was a passerby on the street observing you as you did it, I may not know what it was that you were doing, but I would know by your behavior that there was something specific you were trying to accomplish in that moment.

So, if you relate this to Wilma as she sits and swings, this may lead you to a few ideas about what she might be doing while she is alone. The difference is that, while multiplying the two numbers had no real importance to you, what Wilma is doing would have meaning to HER. And, all of this must lead to what you are actually doing while you are sitting alone at the beginning of this scene. Whatever it is that you are doing, it must have meaning to who? That's right. To you.

Ok, get to work!

1. COMPARE THE SCENE TO THE EXERCISE:

a) Who is in the room?

_____

_____

b) What is her activity?

_____

_____

c) Who is coming to the door?

_____

_____

d) What is bringing her to the door?

_____

_____

e) What is their relationship?

_____

_____

2. WHAT IS THE EMOTIONAL PREPARATION

Wilma:

_____

_____

_____

_____

_____

_____

_____

Arabella:

_____

_____

_____

_____

_____

_____

_____

3. WHAT IS OF IMPORTANCE TO EACH CHARACTER

WILMA

_____

_____

_____

_____

_____

_____

_____

_____

_____

_____

_____

_____

_____

_____

_____

_____

_____

_____

_____

_____

_____

_____

WILMA

_____

_____

_____

_____

_____

_____

_____

_____

_____

_____

_____

_____

_____

_____

_____

_____

_____

_____

_____

_____

_____

_____

_____

_____

ARABELLA

ARABELLA

4. WORK WITH YOUR PARTNER!

Now you may continue with your series of mechanical readings, working readings, learning the words by rote, adding repetition, putting the scene on its feet and then having a full improvisation with the scene.

. . .

what's next!

As you learned here, the script is your bible. And that's what book four will be all about. How to be inspired and nourished by the text and how to investigate it in personal and creative ways. I will teach you how to ask the vital questions of interpretation so that your unique voice comes shining through as you bring to life that elusive thing we call "the character."

We will cover in depth things like:

- personalizing the text,
- text journal work,
- breaking down the script,
- making active choices,
- "doings,"
- "as-ifs," and
- other key elements of interpratation.

You will learn how to really "know" what you are talking about on stage and how to bring yourself in personal allignment with the character's own very specific point of view.

And this one is worth saying again — you will learn how to become authentically and passionately active as you begin to fully understand that on stage, every word out of your mouth is an "activity" because every word that comes out of your mouth is necessary and is a result of something essential you are *trying to accomplish* in each moment!

You know, everything we have done together in the first three books has been the groundwork for what we will work on together in book four. This next part is the huge piece of acting most actors don't want to deal with because it is painstaking work. But I'll tell ya, it is the most rewarding and satisfying part. It is the part that really makes sense of everything else we have so rigorously grappled with. It is the part that allows your instincts to soar and puts you into the domain of "artist."

I get turned on just talking about it. See you there!

Love, Larry

A THANK YOU

I have received so many wonderful telephone calls and letters with reactions to my first two Meisner Approach books and I want all of you to know that you inspire me and help me keep writing. What a gift it has been to hear from you with questions about the exercises, with your experiences of doing the work and to know that you have found my books useful and meaningful in your lives! Truly, I could not have done this new book without all of you.

Please feel free to contact me. I'd love to know if you actually worked on any of the scenes in this book with an acting partner and what your experience was! Also, if you are a teacher using the book in your classes, I'd love to hear how things went with your students and their learning this process of scene-work as well as what it was like for you to witness them working in this manner. Here is my address and phone number:

Larry Silverberg
Acting Enterprises
PO Box 16205
Seattle, WA 98116
(206) 781-7305

BIOGRAPHY

Larry Silverberg, author of *The Sanford Meisner Approach: An Actor's Workbook, The Sanford Meisner Approach: Workbook Two — Emotional Freedom, The Sanford Meisner Approach: Workbook Three — Tackling the Text, Loving To Audition, The Actor's Guide to Qualified Acting Coaches: New York* and *The Actor's Guide to Qualified Acting Coaches: Los Angeles*, is a graduate of the Neighborhood Playhouse School of Theatre in New York City where he studied with master acting teacher Sanford Meisner. Since then, he has worked professionally as an actor and director throughout the United States and Canada in feature films, network television, Off-Broadway and regional theatre.

Larry also teaches professional acting classes at his own acting studio in Seattle and he has taught master classes in the Meisner work at universities, colleges and acting studios around the country. His students have gone on to work in television and feature films including: *Cape Fear, Making Mr. Right, Let It Ride, Miami Vice, Northern Exposure, B.L. Stryker, Miami Blues, Super Boy, Phantom of the Ritz, America's Most Wanted* and many others.

Larry offers visiting acting intensives and workshops. You may contact him with questions about teaching at your school or with questions about this book at the below address.

Larry is the founder and Artistic Director of the Belltown Theatre Center in Seattle, Washington. His address is: PO Box 16205, Seattle, WA, 98116. (206) 781-7305.

The SANFORD MEISNER *Approach*

The best-selling workbook that opens the door to Meisner's Approach

"Here, Silverberg, who was a student of the master teacher, presents a workbook for actors that will prove useful, regardless of how familiar the reader is with Meisner's methods. Silverberg's writing is concise and insightful throughout and makes the technique accessible to any committed student." —*Library Journal*

"For serious theatre students, this book could be highly influential in laying a foundation for their acting careers."
—*Voice of Youth Advocates*

both books include specific exercises from the Method

WORKBOOK ONE: AN ACTOR'S WORKBOOK
ISBN 1-880399-77-6
176 pages, $12.95

WORKBOOK TWO: EMOTIONAL FREEDOM
ISBN 1-57525-074-8
116 pages, $14.95

Published by Smith and Kraus
*available at your local bookstore
or call 1.800.895.4331*

The Actor's Guide to Qualified Acting Coaches

by Larry Silverberg

VOLUME I: NEW YORK
VOLUME II: LOS ANGELES

*Finding the right acting coaches to work with, those
you can trust and learn from, those who are best
suited for your own skill levels and career goals, can be
an overwhelming undertaking. Now there's help!*

The Actor's Guide to Qualified Acting Coaches
*will lead you to the finest acting teachers in New York
and Los Angeles through penetrating interviews
with teachers and their students.*

New York Volume
ISBN 1-57525-009-8
160 pages $11.95

Los Angeles Volume
ISBN 1-57525-010-1
160 pages $11.95

Published by Smith and Kraus
*at your local bookstore or
call 1.800.895.4331*

Loving to Audition

The Audition Workbook for Actors
by Larry Silverberg

"A valuable, adventurous, and enthusiastic entrée into the little defined world of auditioning."
Allan Miller, actor, director, teacher, and author

"Acting coach Larry Silverberg takes two monologues and proceeds for 147 pages to dissect every word, every possible layer of meaning, every possible angle of approach, to show how a master actor would interpret the speeches at an audition. Silverberg supplies so many techniques for climbing inside the brief texts that any actor with the presence of mind to recall a tenth of them in the heat of a real-life audition would have the basis for ample calm confidence. This is a really useful guide for absorbing text quickly — whether for performer or audience."

*Drama, Dance, and Theater Editor's
Recommended Book, Amazon.com*

includes specific exercises
LOVING TO AUDITION
ISBN 1-57525-007-1
144 pages, $15.95

Published by Smith and Kraus
*available at your local bookstore
or call 1.800.895.4331*